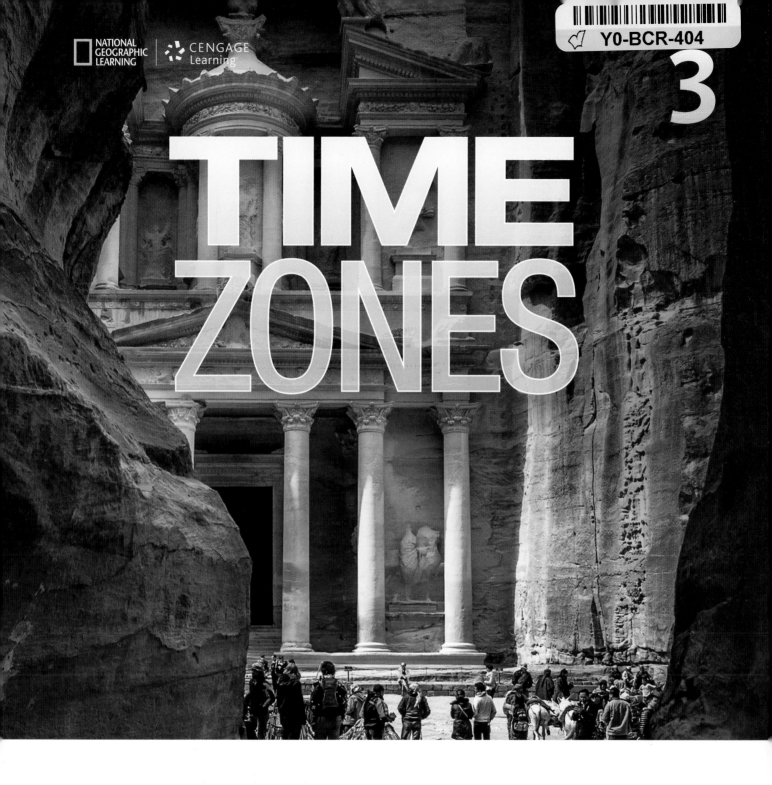

NATIONAL GEOGRAPHIC LEARNING | CENGAGE Learning

TIME ZONES

3

David Bohlke
Jennifer Wilkin

SECOND EDITION

NATIONAL GEOGRAPHIC LEARNING | CENGAGE Learning

Australia • Brazil • Japan • Korea • Mexico • Singapore • Spain • United Kingdom • United States

Time Zones Student Book 3
Second Edition

David Bohlke and Jennifer Wilkin

Publisher: Andrew Robinson

Senior Development Editor: Derek Mackrell

Development Editors: Sian Mavor,
Charlotte Sharman

Associate Development Editor:
Ridhima Thakral

Director of Global Marketing: Ian Martin

Product Marketing Manager: Anders Bylund

Media Researcher: Leila Hishmeh

Senior Director of Production:
Michael Burggren

Senior Content Project Manager:
Tan Jin Hock

Manufacturing Planner:
Mary Beth Hennebury

Compositor: Cenveo Publisher Services

Cover/Text Design: Creative Director:
Christopher Roy, Art Director: Scott Baker,
Senior Designer: Michael Rosenquest

Cover Photo: Al Khazneh (the Treasury), Petra,
Jordan: Boom Chuthai/500px Prime

Student Book with Online Workbook:
ISBN-13: 978-1-305-51073-9

Student Book:
ISBN-13: 978-1-305-25986-7

National Geographic Learning
20 Channel Center Street
Boston, MA 02210
USA

Cengage Learning is a leading provider of customized learning solutions with employees residing in nearly 40 different countries and sales in more than 125 countries around the world. Find your local representative at:
www.cengage.com

Cengage Learning products are represented in Canada by Nelson Education, Ltd.

Visit National Geographic Learning online at **NGL.Cengage.com**

Visit our corporate website at **www.cengage.com**

Printed in China
Print Number: 08   Print Year: 2019

Contents

SCOPE AND SEQUENCE

4

WHICH ONE IS
JUSTIN?

Preview

A 🎧1–01 **Listen.** Matt is telling a new student about the people in the photo. Label them with the correct letters.

> a. Justin   b. Adam   c. Chris   d. Taylor

B 🎧1–01 **Listen again and match.** What is each student like?

1. Justin ○   ○ a. really funny
2. Adam ○   ○ b. pretty easygoing
3. Chris ○   ○ c. quiet and a little shy
4. Taylor ○   ○ d. really hard-working

C **Talk with a partner.** Identify the people in the photo. Use the phrases in the box or your own ideas.

> holding a helmet   wearing a backpack
> wearing a belt   holding a green book
> holding a tablet   wearing black jeans

Taylor is the one who's holding a green book.

And Adam is the one who's wearing . . .

Language Focus

A 🎧1-02 **Listen and read.** Then repeat the conversation and replace the words in blue.

B **Practice with a partner.** Replace any words to make your own conversation.

REAL ENGLISH Hang on.

1 Thanks for coming with me to **meet** my cousin Ursula.

No problem. I remember you telling me about your cousins.

get
pick up

2 Is Ursula the one who **lives in Los Angeles**?

No, that's my cousin Ingrid.

works in Hollywood
recently moved to L.A.

3 So what's Ursula like?

Well, she's **very outgoing**. And she's tall and stylish, like me!

really funny
a lot of fun

4 There she is! Welcome! I'm Ming. **May I take your bag?**

Hang on, Ming. This isn't Ursula. *That's* Ursula!

Can I help you with your bag?
Let me help you with your bag.

🎧1-03

DESCRIBING PEOPLE

What's Justin **like**?	He's quiet and a little shy.
Which one is Taylor?	She's **the one with** the long black hair. She's **the one in** the green T-shirt. She's **the one who's** holding a coffee.
Which ones are your cousins?	They're **the ones** near the door. They're **the ones who are** laughing.

C **Complete the sentences.** Use the words from the box.

> patient   chatty   dependable   shy   funny

1. Marissa is always talking to someone. She's really _____.

2. Walt doesn't feel comfortable around other people. He's pretty _____.

3. Hee-jin is always there when her friends need her. She's so _____.

4. Michael makes all of his friends laugh. He's very _____.

5. Patricia never gets upset when she has to wait in line. She's extremely _____.

D (1-04) **Join the sentences with *who*.** Then listen and check.

1. That's Akio. He likes to sit in the first row.

   _Akio is the one who likes to sit in the first row_____.

2. Her name is Suzy. She's sitting next to Akio.

   _____.

3. That's Eric and that's Michael. They like to ask a lot of questions.

   _____.

4. Her name is Sonia. She always brings her tablet to class.

   _____.

E **Work with a partner. Student A:** Go to page 126. **Student B:** Go to page 129. You are going to identify people at a party.

The Big Picture

Max Lowe is a National Geographic Explorer. Before he could even walk, Lowe was going on adventures with his parents as they traveled the world. From Montana to Mongolia, Lowe now captures people and places across the globe with his camera.

A 🎧1-05 **Listen to the interview.** Check (✓) the things Lowe talks about.

- ☐ his hometown
- ☐ his school life
- ☐ his first digital camera
- ☐ his future plans
- ☐ his hobbies
- ☐ his heroes

B 🎧1-05 **Listen again.** Circle **T** for True or **F** for False.

1. Lowe studied journalism in college.   **T**   **F**

2. Lowe mentions three people who are his heroes.   **T**   **F**

3. Lowe's father is the one who introduced him to the outdoors.   **T**   **F**

4. Lowe says it's challenging to truly understand and tell someone's story.   **T**   **F**

Discussion. Lowe describes his heroes as inspiring. What characteristics do you think are important in a hero?

Pronunciation
Syllable stress

A 🎧1–06 **Listen and repeat.** Notice the stressed syllables.

First syllable	Second syllable	Third syllable
patient	ex**plor**er	intro**duce**
picture	in**spir**ing	geo**graph**ic
national	psy**chol**ogist	conver**sa**tion

B 🎧1–07 **Underline the stress in the words in bold.** Then listen and check your answers.

1. Should a **hero** be **dependable**?

2. Are you an **introvert** or an **extrovert**?

3. Do you **enjoy** outdoor **activities**?

4. Who's someone who is **easygoing** and **talkative**?

5. What **information** do you **remember** about Lowe?

C **Work with a partner.** Take turns to ask and answer the questions in **B**.

DO YOU KNOW?

People who are talkative and outgoing are called _____.

a. introverts
b. extroverts

Communication

A **Play a guessing game.** Write four things about yourself on four pieces of paper. Fold them in half. Don't show anyone!

> I'm talkative and outgoing.

> I like Taylor Swift.

> I'm good at computer games.

> I take piano lessons.

B **Work with a group.** Put the papers on a table. Then take turns choosing a paper and guessing who wrote it. When you guess correctly, keep the paper.

> I think Kenji is the one who takes piano lessons.

> Sorry! It's not me.

Willie (on Megan's arm) with Hannah and her mom

Reading

A **Read the title.** What do you think the article is about?

B **Predict.** What kind of animal is each pet?

1. Willie _____ 2. Buddy _____ 3. Winnie _____

C **Skim the text.** What did each animal do? Match.

1. Willie ○   ○ a. woke up its owner to warn of danger.

2. Buddy ○   ○ b. alerted the babysitter that someone needed help.

3. Winnie ○   ○ c. made an emergency phone call.

LIFE SAVERS

🎧1–08

Willie the parrot saved the life of two-year-old Hannah Kuusk. The young child was eating when something got stuck in her throat. Hannah's babysitter, Megan Howard, was in the bathroom at the time. She suddenly heard the bird screaming and making noises
5 with its wings. "Then he started saying 'mama baby' over and over and over again until I came out," Howard said. Howard saw that Hannah's face was blue. Howard was quickly able to remove the food from Hannah's throat, but she says that Willie is the real hero. Willie was the one who later received an award for saving Hannah's life!

10 When he was eight weeks old, Buddy the German shepherd came to live with Joe Stalnaker. Stalnaker suffers from seizures—sudden attacks that make him unable to move easily. Stalnaker taught his new dog to bring him the phone when he started to experience a seizure. Stalnaker also trained Buddy to hit the speed dial button on
15 the phone to call 911. So when Stalnaker had a really bad seizure, Buddy was the one who called for help and began making sounds into the phone. Emergency rescue workers arrived within minutes and found Stalnaker. They took him to the hospital where he recovered. Stalnaker later said this about Buddy: "He's my world. He's
20 my best friend, no question. He's always there, and I just hope I can be as good to him as he's been to me."

One night, a gas-powered water pump at the Keesling home began to leak. The family was sleeping. Their cat, Winnie, began to push her owners and made loud meowing sounds. "It was a crazy meow,
25 almost like she was screaming," said Cathy Keesling. Keesling woke up and was already feeling sick. It was hard for her to wake up her husband and son because they already breathed in a large amount of gas. But thanks to their heroic cat Winnie, Keesling was able to call 911 and get help before anyone was hurt. The family says that
30 Winnie is the one who saved their lives.

Comprehension

(A) **Answer the questions about *Life Savers*.**

1. [Detail] Which pets saved their owners' lives?

   a. Buddy

   b. Buddy and Winnie

   c. Buddy, Willie, and Winnie

2. [Inference] Hannah was blue because she ____.

   a. was hungry

   b. was cold

   c. couldn't breathe

3. [Detail] When Stalnaker had a really bad seizure, Buddy called ____.

   a. Stalnaker's friend

   b. 911

   c. the hospital

4. [Paraphrase] "He's my world" means "He's ____."

   a. like a hero

   b. a good dog

   c. everything to me

5. [Inference] Winnie made such a loud meow sound because she was ____.

   a. trying to wake up Cathy

   b. not able to sleep

   c. feeling sick

IDIOM

An "unsung" hero is a hero who ____.

a. cannot sing
b. isn't famous
c. hates being a hero

(B) **Sequence the events.** For each story, number the events from 1 to 4 in the order they happened.

Willie	◯ Willie started to scream.	◯ Willie said "mama baby" over and over.
	◯ Howard removed the stuck food.	◯ Food got stuck in Hannah's throat.
Buddy	◯ Buddy called 911.	◯ Stalnaker suffered a bad seizure.
	◯ Emergency rescue workers arrived.	◯ Stalnaker taught Buddy to hit speed dial.
Winnie	◯ Keesling called 911.	◯ Cathy's husband and son woke up.
	◯ A water pump began to leak.	◯ Winnie started to meow loudly.

(C) **CRITICAL THINKING** **Talk with a partner.** Which animal in the article do you think is the most heroic? Do you know any other animals that saved their owners' lives?

Writing

Write a blog about someone who inspires you.

Home   BLOG   Photos   Contact   About Me

My grandmother is very hardworking and serious, but she is also very outgoing and funny. She often takes me on short hiking trips. She is 78 years old and has a lot of energy. My grandmother is the one who took care of me when I was sick last year. She hardly ever left my side. . . .

Mountain People

ABOUT THE VIDEO

The Sherpa live high in the mountains of Nepal.

BEFORE YOU WATCH

Guess. What do you know about Sherpas? Circle **T** for True or **F** for False.

1. Sherpas live in the Himalayas.   T   F

2. The name Sherpa means "western people."   T   F

3. Many Sherpas work as mountain guides.   T   F

WHILE YOU WATCH

A **Check your answers to the Before You Watch question.**

B **Watch the video again.** Circle the words you hear.

1. Edmund Hillary was from (**Australia** / **New Zealand**).

2. Tenzing Norgay became famous after (**1953** / **1973**).

3. Kancha Sherpa says the recent changes in Sherpa lives are (**bad** / **good**).

4. Kancha Sherpa's only worry is (**global warming** / **earning money**).

AFTER YOU WATCH

Talk with a partner. Would you like to climb a high mountain? Why or why not?

A sherpa climbs down the Khumbu Ice Fall, Nepal

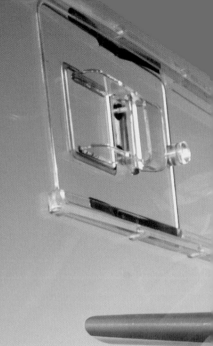

2

I'D LIKE TO BE A PILOT.

Preview

A 🎧 **1-09** **Listen to a teacher and her students discuss jobs.** Circle the kind of job each student wants.

1. Katie wants a job that (**is challenging** / **lets her travel**). ○ ○ a. singer

2. Micah wants a job that (**is fun** / **lets him work with computers**). ○ ○ b. chef

3. Laura wants a job that (**is dangerous** / **lets her be creative**). ○ ○ c. accountant

4. Miguel wants a job that (**is exciting** / **lets him help people**). ○ ○ d. pilot

5. Wendy wants a job that (**pays well** / **lets her work with animals**). ○ ○ e. doctor

B **CRITICAL THINKING** 🎧 **1-10** **Guess.** Match the student with the job he or she wants. Then listen and check your answers.

C **Talk with a partner.** What other jobs can you name for each description in **A**?

> What other jobs are fun?

> I know. An actor!

A pilot flies upside down over Maryland, U.S.A.

Language Focus

A 🎧 1–11 **Listen and read.** Then repeat the conversation and replace the words in blue.

REAL ENGLISH Why don't you . . . ?

B **Practice with a partner.** Replace any words to make your own conversation.

1 What kind of job do you want, Maya?

I want a job that **lets me travel**.

lets me be creative
pays a lot of money

2 Like **a flight attendant**?

No, I'd like to do something that's more exciting.

a chef
an app developer

3 Why don't you become **a pilot**?

Hmmm . . . I don't know.

a photographer
a lawyer

4 THANK YOU FOR COMING

So what *would* you like to be?

Actually, I just want to **travel**. I don't really want a job!

see new places
have a lot of money

🎧 1–12

TALKING ABOUT CAREER GOALS	
What kind of job do you want? What kind of job would you like?	I want a job **that lets me work with animals**. **I'd like** a job **that pays a lot of money**. I wouldn't like a job **that's dangerous**.
What **do** you **want to be** someday? What **would** you **like to do** someday?	I **want to be** a doctor. **I'd like to work** as a doctor.

C **Complete the sentences.** Use *that* and phrases from the box.

> ~~creative~~   travel   work with animals
>
> dangerous   pay a lot of money   perform on stage

1. Rachel would like to be an art teacher, because she wants a job _that lets her be creative_ .

2. Brian doesn't want to be a police officer. He doesn't want a job _____ .

3. Both Mia and Joe want to work in finance, because they want jobs _____ .

4. I want to be a flight attendant, because I want a job _____ .

5. Carrie wants to be a singer or dancer. She'd like a job _____ .

6. I'd like to be a vet someday, because I want a job _____ .

D **1-13** **Complete the conversation.** Circle the correct words. Listen and check.

Robert: Look at this app, Sami. You put in information about yourself and it recommends a job for you.

Sami: What kind of information?

Robert: Well, I said I want a job that (1) (**let** / **lets**) me work (2) (**with** / **as**) computers. I also said I like to work (3) (**with** / **as**) numbers.

Sami: So what job does it recommend?

Robert: An accountant. But I don't really want to work (4) (**with** / **as**) an accountant. It's so boring.

Sami: So, what (5) (**do** / **would**) you like to do?

Robert: I (6) (**want** / **would**) to work (7) (**with** / **as**) an app developer. I'd (8) (**like** / **want**) to develop apps, but apps that are better than this one!

E **Play a game.** Think of a job. Other students take turns asking yes/no questions to try to guess the job. Then switch roles.

> Is the job dangerous?

> Is it a job that lets you work outside?

> Is it a job that pays a lot of money?

> Is it a job that's popular with young people?

Fun Jobs

Some people have jobs that are not only exciting, but also fun! Meet three people with unusual jobs and find out what you need to get these jobs.

Sean Kenney—a LEGO artist—working in his studio

A 🎧 1–14 **Listen to descriptions of three fun jobs.** Choose the best description for each job.

1. Seb Smith ___ water slides.
   a. rides and rates   b. designs

2. Sean Kenney ___ LEGO bricks.
   a. paints   b. builds things using

3. Tracy Lewis ___ at a theme park.
   a. acts on stage   b. wears a costume

B **CRITICAL THINKING** 🎧 1–15 **Guess.** Match two qualities that would help someone get each job. Listen and check.

Water slide tester ○   ○ can write well
                                ○ can work hard

LEGO artist ○   ○ is creative
                                ○ is confident

Character performer ○   ○ is flexible
                                ○ is friendly

Discussion. Tell your partner what job you would love to do.

Pronunciation
Sentence stress

A 🎧 1–16 **Listen and repeat.** Notice how the most important words are stressed.

1. She **dresses** up as **characters** at a **theme park**.

2. **Doctors** and **nurses like** to **help people**.

3. I **want** a **job** that **lets** me **work** with **animals**.

B 🎧 1–17 **Underline the important words in each sentence.** Then listen and circle the stressed words.

1. Dani wants a job that lets her work with children.

2. An accountant is someone who is good with numbers.

3. Sun-hee wants a job that's challenging and exciting.

4. The chef is the one who cooks your food in a restaurant.

C **Work with a partner.** Take turns to read the sentences in **B**.

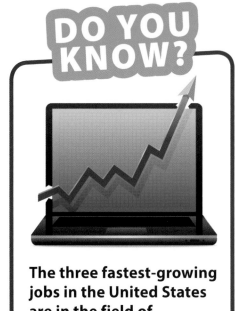

DO YOU KNOW?

The three fastest-growing jobs in the United States are in the field of _____.

a. arts and entertainment
b. health care
c. the environment

Communication

Interview your partner. Add three more ideas to the chart. Check (✓) the kind of job your partner wants to have. Then give some career advice.

> Do you want a job that lets you work outside?

> You should be an animal trainer. You shouldn't be an app developer.

lets you work outside	
is interesting and exciting	
lets you work with animals	
has regular hours	
lets you use social media	
requires you to speak English	
pays a lot of money	

A seal trainer in Szeged Zoo, Hungary

Reading

A **Read the title.** What does the word "extreme" mean?

B **Scan the first and the fourth paragraphs.** What two jobs do the women do? Which job do you think is more extreme? Why?

C **Read the text.** Underline other jobs that are mentioned.

Wang Yaping was the second Chinese woman to travel to space.

EXTREME JOBS

🎧 1–18

Katy Croff Bell likes extremes. As an oceanographer, she often explores the deepest parts of the ocean. Her days are long and tiring. She can sometimes spend weeks or months on a research ship. "We work in shifts to collect data 24 hours a day," says Bell. "We typically
5 work day and night with very little sleep." But Bell isn't complaining.

She often works with Robert Ballard, the oceanographer who found *Titanic* in 1985. Together, they explore the most remote parts of our planet. Bell uses the latest video technology and deep sea robotic vehicles to connect with hundreds of scientists and students all over
10 the world. These students then get to watch live videos from the bottom of the ocean, and get to study subjects like geology and archeology in real time.

Bell chose ocean exploration as a career after she went to sea for the first time in 1999. "My first seagoing experience changed my life," she
15 says. "And I hope to use the excitement of exploration to inspire a new generation of young explorers."

Wang Yaping has a job that lets her travel—all the way to space. Wang is an astronaut. In 2013, Wang became the second Chinese woman to travel to space. She was a member of the Shenzhou 10
20 spaceship crew and a member of the Tiangong-1 space station. While on Tiangong-1, China described her as its first teacher in space. She taught a physics class to Chinese students, in real time, by a live TV broadcast. She spent more than two weeks in space before returning home a national hero.

25 Wang had to go through an intense three-year training to prepare for life in space. "I think the training has helped me grow up . . . and fully embrace teamwork with my crewmates," she said.

Wang remembers how she felt when the first Chinese astronaut went into space 10 years before her. She was watching it on TV.
30 "I was so proud and also very excited. But as I watched it, it occurred to me: We have male pilots and female pilots. And then a male astronaut. When will there be a female astronaut? And today, it's me becoming one of the first few."

Comprehension

A **Answer the questions about *Extreme Jobs*.**

1. `Inference` Which of the following statements about Bell is NOT true?

   a. She found *Titanic* with Ballard.

   b. She likes adventures.

   c. She thinks exploration is exciting.

2. `Vocabulary` What does the word "typically" mean? (line 4)

   a. always

   b. without stopping

   c. usually

3. `Inference` Bell chose ocean exploration as a career because she ____.

   a. thought it was exciting

   b. wanted to change her life

   c. wanted to find *Titanic*

4. `Detail` Which statement about Wang is true?

   a. She spent over two months in space.

   b. She taught physics from space.

   c. She is the first Chinese woman to travel to space.

5. `Detail` What inspired Wang to become an astronaut?

   a. taking a physics class

   b. learning the importance of teamwork

   c. seeing China's first astronaut in space on TV

IDIOM

An example of a "nine-to-five" job is ____ .

a. a truck driver
b. an accountant
c. a dancer

B **Complete. Write B for Bell, W for Wang, and B, W for both.**

1. has an exciting job ____

2. explores the deepest oceans ____

3. can spend months on a research ship at one time ____

4. has a job that lets her travel ____

5. underwent three years of training ____

6. uses technology to teach students ____

C **CRITICAL THINKING** **Talk with a partner.** Which job did you say was more extreme in **Reading B**? Do you still feel that way? What qualities do you think a person needs to do extreme jobs like this?

Writing

Write a letter to a guidance counselor. Describe yourself. Ask about different jobs and careers.

March 29

Dear Mr. Chen,

I would like some information about different jobs. I am good at art and math. I really like to make things, so I would like a job that lets me be creative. . . .

Wildfire Photographer

ABOUT THE VIDEO

National Geographic photographer Mark Thiessen spends his vacation photographing wildfires.

BEFORE YOU WATCH

Guess. What do you think it's like to be a wildfire photographer? Circle the statements you think you will hear in the video.

It's sometimes dangerous.	It pays well.
It has regular hours.	It lets you be creative.
It lets you work with people.	It's challenging.

WHILE YOU WATCH

A Check your answers to the Before You Watch question.

B Watch the video again. Circle the correct answer.

1. Thiessen usually takes photos of (**wild animals / people and things**).

2. Thiessen first wanted to become a photographer when he was (**a child / a university student**).

3. Thiessen takes photos of wildfires every (**summer / fall**).

4. Thiessen thinks the sight of trees damaged by fire can be (**depressing / beautiful**).

AFTER YOU WATCH

Talk with a partner. Would you like to be a photographer? What would you like to take pictures of?

Mark Thiessen photographing a fire on a forest hillside, Montana, U.S.A.

3

PLEASE DON'T FEED THE MONKEYS.

Preview

A 🎧 1–19 **Listen to students learning about rules.** Number the signs (1–4) in the order the rules are discussed.

_____   _____   _____   _____

B 🎧 1–19 **Listen again and match.**

1. You have to turn off your phone in the   ○   ○   a. bus.

2. You can't take photos in the   ○   ○   b. library.

3. You're not allowed to eat or drink on the ○   ○   c. movie theater.

4. You have to be quiet in the   ○   ○   d. museum.

C **Talk with a partner.** What are some other rules around town?

> You have to take off your shoes in the temple.

> You can't be in the park after 10:00 p.m.

PLEASE DO NOT FEED THE MONKEYS

A monkey sitting near a sign, Kuala Lumpur, Malaysia

Language Focus

A 🎧1-20 **Listen and read.** Then repeat the conversation and replace the words in blue.

REAL ENGLISH   kind of

B **Practice with a partner.** Replace any words to make your own conversation.

1 How's your new part-time job at the movie theater, Nadine?

It's **awesome**. I love it!

great
fantastic

2 Are you allowed to use your phone at work?

Sure. My boss doesn't mind.

Can you talk on the phone? Is this a good time to talk?

3 Cool! Can you watch the movies and **eat popcorn**?

Yes, I can!

eat the candy
drink soda

4 Wow—it sounds fun! Do you have to wear a uniform?

Kind of, but it's **really cool**.

very stylish
a really pretty uniform

🎧 1-21

TALKING ABOUT RULES	
Can you talk on the phone at work?	Yes, I **can** (talk on the phone). No, I **can't** (talk on the phone).
Are you **allowed** to use your phone?	Yes, I **am** (**allowed to** use my phone). No, I'**m not** (**allowed to** use my phone).
Do you **have to** wear a uniform?	Yes, I do. / Yes, I **have to** (wear a uniform). No, I **don't** (**have to** wear a uniform).

C **Read the rules.** Rewrite them using *can't* or *have to*.

1. _____ .

2. _____ .

3. _____ .

4. _____ .

5. _____ .

6. _____ .

1. Don't walk on the grass.
2. Stay on the path.
3. Don't feed the animals.
4. Don't play loud music.
5. Recycle your bottles.
6. Walk your bike.

D 🎧1–22 **Complete the conversations.** Write the correct words. Listen and check.

1. Adam: _____ you _____ your bike at the bus stop? (**allowed to / park**)

   Joe: Yes, but you _____ it in the parking lot next to the stop. (**have to / put**)

2. Justin: _____ you _____ your own laptop to the library? (**have to / bring**)

   Taylor: No, you _____ . (**not have to**) There are computers in the study room.

3. Megan: _____ you _____ the bike path in the park for running? (**can / use**)

   Walt: Well, you _____ (**allowed to / run**) on it, but it's really for bikes.

4. Jenny: _____ I _____ (**have to / get**) a ticket before I get on the bus?

   Carlos: No, you _____ (**can / buy**) one from the driver.

5. Max: You _____ (**not allowed to / listen to**) music here.

   Lucy: Oh, I'm sorry.

E **Think about the rules in your school, home, or another place.** Write three true and three false rules. Then share them in a group. Can the others guess the false rules?

> You're not allowed to drink in the computer lab.

> I think that's true.

The Real World

Is That Real?

Wherever we are, we have to follow rules. Rules help to keep everyone safe. Some rules, however, sound strange at first! Here are some unusual rules from different countries around the world.

Slow Down
Deer
Crossing

North Vancouver District

A **What do you think these signs mean?** Check (✓) the signs you think are real.

1. _____   2. _____   3. _____   4. _____

5. _____   6. _____   7. _____   8. _____

(Turn to page 129 for answers.)

B 🎧 1-23 **Listen to some unusual rules.** Complete each rule. Listen again and check.

1. In Thailand, you aren't allowed to step on (**money / books**).

2. In Greece, women in (**high heels / leather clothing**) can't go inside monuments.

3. In Italy, you can't feed the (**pigeons / cats**) in St. Mark's Square, Venice.

4. In Spain, you can't drive a car (**if you are under 25 / while wearing flip flops**).

5. In Canada, one in every five songs on the radio must be sung by a (**Canadian / woman**).

Discussion. Which rule do you think is the most surprising? Are there any unusual rules in your country?

Pronunciation

Reduction: *has to* and *have to*

A 🎧1–24 **Listen to the sentences.** Notice how *has to* is pronounced /hasta/ and *have to* is pronounced /hafta/.

1. My sister **has to** take her lunch to school.

2. In some countries, students **have to** go to school on Saturdays.

B 🎧1–25 **Listen and complete the sentences.**

1. My little brother _____ to bed at 8:00.

2. What do you _____ this week?

3. I _____ a presentation at the science fair.

4. We _____ uniforms at our school.

5. I don't _____ in my room.

6. My sister _____ her homework every day.

C **Work with a partner.** Take turns to read the sentences in **B**.

DO YOU KNOW?

In Germany, what is the upper speed limit on the autobahn (highway)?

a. 60 km/h
b. 120 km/h
c. There's no speed limit.

Communication

A **Make rules for a club.** Work in groups. Find an interest you all share (e.g. music, sports, art, languages). Form an after-school club. Give your club a name and decide on four rules.

> What rules do we need for our comic book club?

> One could be, "You're not allowed to argue."

B **Make signs.** Draw four signs for your club rules.

C **Share your signs with another group.** Can they guess the rules? Do they want to join?

Reading

A **Look at the photos and the title.** What do you think the article is about?

B **Match.** Match the captions (a–d) to the correct photos (1–4).

    a. Red barn against the sky _____
           c. Morning exercise in Shanghai _____

    b. Two women _____
                       d. Amish women on the beach _____

C **Scan.** In your notebook, write all the words that mean "photo."

1. Most photographers say never point your camera directly into the sun—the light has to come from behind. In this photo, the sun is behind the dancers, making a beautiful image. However, you still have to avoid shooting directly at the sun or all you will see in the photo is bright light.

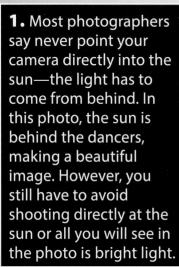

3. Another rule of photography is to leave empty space for people to move into. This is called the active space rule. Try doing the opposite. Photograph people moving *away* from the space, like in this photo. This creates an illusion: the women leave something behind.

BREAKING the RULES

🎧 1–26

To be a good photographer, is it important to learn the basic rules of photography? Many people say yes: There are certain rules that professional photographers follow. But are you 5 allowed to break the rules? What happens when you do? Often, you get a more creative, interesting image. So the next time you snap a pic, don't be afraid to try one of these techniques. You might just get the perfect shot!

2. Photographers say the main subject of your photograph should always be in focus. The focus on secondary details in the scene are not as important. Here, the main subject is out of focus. The layered effect creates a sense of peeking behind the scenes. This makes for an interesting image.

4. When you take pictures of the outdoors, photographers say to keep lines straight. But in this photo of a barn, the photographer decided to turn the camera and point it up. This creates an unusual angle. The scene changes from something that is expected to something that is surprising.

Comprehension

A **Answer the questions about *Breaking the Rules*.**

1. `Main Idea` The reading is about how breaking rules can make _____ .

   a. photos look more interesting

   b. photography difficult

   c. photos look poor

2. `Detail` Which of these would make a poor photo? Shooting _____ .

   a. with light behind you

   b. with light behind the subject

   c. directly into the sun

3. `Inference` Most photographers _____ .

   a. focus on the main subject

   b. pay more attention to secondary details

   c. try to create a layered effect

4. `Detail` The active space rule says you should leave empty space for people to _____ .

   a. move into

   b. move away from

   c. create an illusion

5. `Inference` To create an element of surprise you should _____ .

   a. take pictures outdoors

   b. keep lines straight

   c. create an unusual angle

> **IDIOM**
>
> **If you do something "by the book," you _____ .**
>
> a. follow all the rules
> b. break all the rules
> c. read all the rules

B **Sort.** Write **R** for the rules photographers follow and **B** for rules that they've broken.

Turn the camera and point it upwards. _____   Leave space for people to move into. _____

Point your camera directly into the light. _____   Shoot with the light behind you. _____

Focus on the main subject of the photo. _____   Keep lines straight. _____

C **CRITICAL THINKING** **Work in a group.** Find a photo in this book that you like. Then explain why. Do you think the photographer broke any rules?

Writing

Imagine you are the teacher. Write a short paragraph explaining four rules for your class. State why they are important.

In my class, students have to be on time. They are not allowed to be late. This is important because they might miss part of the class. They also have to turn off their cell phones . . .

Rules of the Road

ABOUT THE VIDEO
Many countries have unusual driving rules.

BEFORE YOU WATCH

Guess. What do the following road signs mean? Discuss with a partner.

WHILE YOU WATCH

A **Check (✓) the countries you hear.**

- ○ Brazil
- ○ Cyprus
- ○ Sweden
- ○ Thailand
- ○ South Africa
- ○ Japan
- ○ Germany
- ○ Russia

B **Watch the video again.** Write the name of the country next to the law.

1. You have to keep your lights on during the day. _____

2. You're not allowed to run out of gas on the highway. _____

3. You're not allowed to eat or drink anything while driving. _____

4. You have to be careful not to splash someone standing near the road. _____

AFTER YOU WATCH

Talk with a partner. What driving rules do you know in your country? Do you think any of these rules should change?

Two people driving a beach buggy on the Skeleton Coast, Namibia

HOW DO SLOTHS
MOVE?

Sloths move very slowly. They spend most of their time eating and sleeping.

Preview

A 🎧 1–27 **Listen.** Match the animals with the places.

1. sloths ○   ○ a. South Africa
2. bees ○   ○ b. the Amazon rain forest
3. owls ○   ○ c. the United States
4. dolphins ○   ○ d. Mexico

B 🎧 1–27 **Listen again.** Complete the sentences with the words in the box.

> quickly   ~~slowly~~   playfully   gracefully   quietly   hard

1. Sloths move ___slowly___ in trees but _____ in water.
2. Bees work very _____ to make honey.
3. Owls wait _____ for their food.
4. Dolphins swim _____ . They jump _____ out of the water.

C **Talk with a partner.** Name other animals that do these things.

> move slowly   sing loudly   run quickly   wait patiently   swim gracefully

I think lions wait patiently.

Language Focus

A 🎧 1-28 **Listen and read.** Then repeat the conversation and replace the words in blue.

B **Practice with a partner.** Replace any words to make your own conversation.

1 Hey, Nadine. What kind of animal do you think I'm like?

Let's see. . . . I know! You're like a dolphin. You're smart and you swim **really well**!

gracefully
quickly

2 What about me, Ming?

I think you're like **a raccoon** because you eat all kinds of strange things!

an owl
a bat

3 What kind of animal am I like?

You're like a bird because you sing **beautifully**. . .

loudly
well

4 Hurry up, Stig! You're moving very slowly today. You're like a **snail**!

Sorry!

turtle
sloth

🎧 1-29

DESCRIBING BEHAVIOR

Sloths are **slow** and **quiet**.	Sloths move **slowly** and **quietly**.	slow > slow**ly**	
Dolphins are **good** swimmers.	Dolphins swim **well**.	easy > eas**ily**	
		bad > bad**ly**	
Bees are **hard** workers.	Bees work **hard**.	good > **well**	
		fast > **fast**	
How does an owl wait?	It waits **patiently**.	hard > **hard**	

C Circle the correct words.

Snowy owls live in the Arctic. It's not 1. (**easy** / **easily**) to find food there, but these 2. (**beautiful** / **beautifully**) birds are very 3. (**good** / **well**) hunters. They patiently wait for their prey. They sit 4. (**quiet** / **quietly**) and wait until they see a mouse, rabbit, or other small animal. Then they move in 5. (**quick** / **quickly**). Snowy owls also hear very 6. (**good** / **well**). This is important when they are trying to find food under the snow.

D 🎧1–30 **Complete the conversation with the correct forms of the words in parentheses.** Then listen and check your answers.

Maya: What are you reading, Stig?

Stig: Oh, it's a book about elephants. Did you know elephants can communicate (1) _____ (**easy**) with other elephants up to eight kilometers away? They make a (2) _____ (**loud**) sound with their trunk.

Maya: So they have a (3) _____ (**good**) sense of hearing?

Stig: Yeah, but their eyesight is (4) _____ (**bad**). I also learned that they don't run. They just walk (5) _____ (**quick**).

Maya: I know something interesting about elephants.

Stig: What's that?

Maya: They swim (6) _____ (**good**). I saw a video of it. It was (7) _____ (**beautiful**).

E **Complete the sentences about yourself.** Then join a group and share the information. Suggest what animal each person is like.

1. I run _____ .

2. I eat _____ .

3. I jump _____ .

4. I swim _____ .

5. I work _____ .

From your answers, I think you're like a rabbit.

Frog Man

Tyrone Hayes is a National Geographic Explorer.
He's a scientist, but he prefers being in the field rather than the lab. He works hard, and is often wet and cold in a muddy lake at 2 a.m.—that's when the frogs come out.

A **Work with a partner.** What do you know about frogs? Check (✓) the statements you think are true. Frogs _____.

- [ ] can change color
- [ ] are a type of fish
- [ ] drink a lot of water
- [ ] never close their eyes
- [ ] can't climb trees
- [ ] only eat plants

(Turn to page 131 for answers.)

B 🎧1–31 **Listen.** Circle **T** for True or **F** for False.

1. Hayes started studying frogs when he was a young boy. **T** **F**

2. The male frogs changed color because of water pollution. **T** **F**

3. The water was dangerous for frogs, but it was safe for humans. **T** **F**

4. Watching these frogs regularly can save human lives. **T** **F**

Discussion. What other animals can tell us about something dangerous? How else do you think animals can help human beings?

Pronunciation

Reduced vowels in unstressed syllables

A 🎧1-32 **Listen and repeat.**

/ə/	/ə/	/ə/	/ə/
an<u>i</u>mal	el<u>e</u>ph<u>a</u>nt	<u>a</u>round	nati<u>o</u>nal

B 🎧1-33 **Underline the reduced vowel in each word.** Then listen and check your answers. Say each word.

easily	water	about	Amazon
important	climate	patiently	desert

C **Work with a partner.** Take turns to read the words in **B**.

DO YOU KNOW?

What is a group of frogs called?

a. a flock of frogs
b. a school of frogs
c. an army of frogs

Communication

Play charades. Work in small groups. Choose one item from each column and act it out. Other students guess the activity. Take turns.

COLUMN A	COLUMN B	COLUMN C
doing karate	quickly	in a snowstorm
making a sandwich	slowly	with a sore foot
fighting	sleepily	on a hot sidewalk
playing the drums	gracefully	underwater
swimming	loudly	with a headache
singing	softly	on a crowded bus
applying sunscreen	happily	with a dog
taking a shower	badly	during a tornado
eating bugs	hungrily	with a heavy backpack
texting	secretly	with a runny nose

Are you fighting gracefully with a runny nose?

No? Are you applying sunscreen quickly underwater?

Reading

A **Discuss.** Look at the title. Do you think animals can be nice? If so, give an example.

B **Skim the text.** Match the sentences.

1. A fox ○   ○ a. gave food to another animal.

2. A chimpanzee ○   ○ b. protected another animal.

3. An elephant ○   ○ c. played with another animal.

4. A hippo ○   ○ d. helped a researcher.

C **Scan the text.** Then underline the opposites for the words below.

> gently   loudly   slowly

A female fox walking along the Flambeau River, U.S.A.

CAN ANIMALS BE NICE?

🎧 1–34

We know people can be nice, but what about animals?

Scientists say that some animals are capable of being nice. Animals that live in groups—like foxes, chimpanzees, and elephants—follow rules. They have to follow rules to get along and to survive. However, 5 animals can act nicely, even when they don't have to. Here are some surprising stories about animal behavior.

Most people usually walk away when someone is unkind to them. Marc Bekoff, a researcher at the University of Colorado, saw a female red fox do just that. The female fox was unhappy because a male fox 10 played roughly with her. When she walked away, the male fox showed her that he wanted to play nicely. He lowered his head and rolled on his back. The female fox gave him another chance, and this time, he played more gently.

Geza Teleki is a scientist who studies chimpanzees in Tanzania. 15 One day, Teleki hiked far away from his campsite. He didn't have any food. Teleki wanted some fruit from a tree, but the tree was too tall. A young chimpanzee watched him curiously as he tried to get something to eat. The chimpanzee climbed the tree, picked the fruit, and gave it to him!

20 An elephant in Kenya hurt his trunk. He needed help because he couldn't put food into his mouth. Researcher Kayhan Ostovar watched silently. He saw the hurt elephant show his sore trunk to a healthy elephant. The healthy elephant didn't need any more information. He took a bush and put it carefully into his new friend's 25 mouth.

Hippos and crocodiles are usually good friends. They hang out together in rivers. But Karen Paolillo, a wildlife expert in Zimbabwe, saw something surprising. One day, a crocodile tried to eat a monkey that was next to a river. A hippo ran quickly to the crocodile and 30 chased it away. Why did the hippo attack the crocodile? Paolillo says hippos sometimes protect other animals from crocodiles.

Comprehension

A **Answer the questions about *Can Animals Be Nice?***

IDIOM

"As wise as a(n) _____ ."
a. owl
b. mouse
c. dolphin

1. **Main Idea** What is the main idea of the reading?

   a. Animals that live in groups follow rules.

   b. Some animals can be nice to other animals.

   c. Most animals are nice to people.

2. **Paraphrase** In line 9, what does "do just that" mean?

   a. be nice

   b. play roughly

   c. walk away

3. **Inference** We can say that Teleki _____ .

   a. is short

   b. hates hiking

   c. could not climb the tree

4. **Detail** Why did the elephant need help?

   a. The tree was too tall.

   b. It could not use its trunk.

   c. It had no food.

5. **Reference** In line 30, what does "it" refer to?

   a. the crocodile

   b. the chimpanzee

   c. the monkey

B **Identify which statements are causes and which are effects.** Circle **C** for Cause or **E** for Effect.

1. The female fox walked away.   **C   E**   The male fox played roughly.   **C   E**

2. Teleki couldn't get fruit.   **C   E**   The chimpanzee gave fruit to Teleki.   **C   E**

3. The elephant hurt his trunk.   **C   E**   The healthy elephant fed the hurt elephant. **C   E**

4. The hippo attacked the crocodile. **C   E**   The crocodile tried to eat a monkey.   **C   E**

C **CRITICAL THINKING** **Work with a partner.** Which animal from the article do you think was the nicest? Why? Can animals be unkind? Can you think of an example?

Writing

Write a short story about an animal that's nice to another animal. Include a description of the animal's behavior.

One day, Cashew the dog hurt his eyes and became blind. He couldn't see. Libby the cat became a guide cat. Now she guides Cashew carefully around the house . . .

44   Unit 4

Monkey Mayhem

ABOUT THE VIDEO

One town in India is full of monkeys called macaques.

BEFORE YOU WATCH

Guess. Circle **T** for True or **F** for False.

1. Most macaques live in Asia.   **T   F**

2. Macaques can swim.   **T   F**

3. Macaques live alone.   **T   F**

WHILE YOU WATCH

A **Check your answers to the Before You Watch questions.**

B **Watch the video again.** Complete these sentences using words from the video.

1. Macaques move _____ to get their lunch.

2. They eat _____ before the fruit seller comes back.

3. They also have fun and play _____.

4. In the forests they can play as _____ as they want.

5. By the end of a busy day, they're all sleeping _____.

AFTER YOU WATCH

Talk with a partner. Do you think these monkeys are naughty? Do you know any other badly behaved animals?

Macaques sit on a monkey temple rooftop, India

5
I'M MEETING FRIENDS LATER.

Preview

A 🎧 1–35 **Listen.** Four students are talking about their weekend plans. Where are they going? Complete the sentences using the words in the box.

airport	science museum
train station	organic farm
mall	farmers' market
movie theater	flea market

1. Maggie is going to the _____.
   She's (**picking apples** / **buying pies**).

2. Omar is going to the _____.
   It's (**showing movies** /**displaying robots**).

3. Lars is going to the _____.
   He's buying a (**tent** / **sleeping bag**).

4. Amy is going to the _____.
   She's (**dropping off** / **picking up**) her grandfather.

B 🎧 1–35 **Listen again.** Circle the reason they are going to each place.

C **Talk with a partner.** What are you doing this weekend?

> What are you doing this weekend?

> I'm meeting my friends at the mall tomorrow morning.

Students in front of a mural at Coronado High School, California

Language Focus

A 🎧 1–36 **Listen and read.** Then repeat the conversation and replace the words in blue.

B **Practice with a partner.** Replace any words to make your own conversation.

1
Hello, Maya? Are you doing anything on Saturday night?

Um, yeah. I'm **seeing a movie** with a friend.

studying
going shopping

2
Hey, Ming. **What are your plans** this Saturday night?

Um, I'm going to a basketball game.

What are you doing
What are you going to do

3
Nadine, do you want to get together on Saturday night? It's my . . .

Sorry, but **I already have plans**. Maybe another time?

I can't make it
I'm busy that night

4
I feel **bad**. Should we tell him we're planning his birthday party?

No, let's keep it a surprise!

terrible
awful

🎧 1–37

TALKING ABOUT FUTURE EVENTS AND FUTURE PLANS

Scheduled future events	Future plans
I **have** a doctor's appointment on Saturday.	I'**m going** to the mall tomorrow.
The flight **gets in** at 9:30 tomorrow.	She'**s picking** apples on Saturday morning.
What time **does** the movie **start**?	What **are** you **doing** later?
It **starts** at 7:00.	I'**m meeting** my grandfather at the airport.

C **Look at the signs.** Then complete the sentences using the words in the box.

GATE 12
Flight
Seoul–Busan
Departure
9:30
Arrival
10:25

| closes | ends | arrives | leaves | opens | starts |

1. Tony's Pizza _____ at 5:00 a.m. and _____ at 11:00 p.m.

2. The flight _____ Seoul at 9:30 and _____ in Busan at 10:25.

3. The movie _____ at 7:15 and _____ at 9:15.

D 🎧1-38 **Complete the conversations.** Then listen and check your answers.

1. Sam: What _____ you _____ (***do***) this weekend?

   Jenny: Not much. I _____ (***meet***) Erin at the mall on Saturday afternoon.
   We _____ (***see***) a movie and then we _____ (***have***) dinner at China Café.

2. Steve: _____ you _____ (***watch***) the play? What time does it start?

   Chris: It _____ (***start***) at 8:00.

3. Fiona: _____ you _____ (***go***) anywhere this weekend?

   Celia: No. I _____ (***stay***) home. Jesse _____ (***come***) over after his class.
   We might watch a movie.

4. David: What time _____ the farmers' market _____ (***open***)?

   Karen: At 9:00. _____ you _____ (***go***)?

E **Work in groups.** Play a memory game. Say what you are doing this weekend.

> This weekend, I'm seeing a movie.

> This weekend, Jared is seeing a movie. I'm going to the farmers' market with my mother.

> This weekend, Jared is seeing a movie. Wendy is going to the farmers' market with her mother. I'm having lunch with Iris. . . .

Crowdfunding

Crowdfunding is a way of raising money for personal or group projects and activities. People usually pick an activity, and a target for the amount of money they want to raise. They then ask people to donate money through a website so that they can reach their target amount.

Kasha interviewing a Mozambican singer in Mozambique

A 🎧1–39 **Listen.** Circle **T** for True or **F** for False.

1. Kasha is traveling alone.	**T**	**F**
2. She started traveling the world when she was 8 years old.	**T**	**F**
3. She's visiting big cities and small villages.	**T**	**F**
4. Kasha met Nap Dow in Myanmar.	**T**	**F**

B 🎧1–39 **Listen again.** Check (✓) the reasons why Kasha wants to travel the world.

- ⃝ to experience life first-hand
- ⃝ to teach people art and life skills
- ⃝ to create a short documentary and book
- ⃝ to raise awareness about global issues

Discussion. Do you think crowdfunding is a good idea? Would you donate money toward Kasha's travel expenses? Why or why not?

Pronunciation
Stress in compound nouns

A 🎧1–40 **Listen and repeat.** Notice how the first noun in compound nouns usually receives more stress.

sunlight	**back**ground	**air**port
art museum	**water** park	**concert** hall

B 🎧1–41 **Listen.** Underline the stressed word in each compound noun.

1. Are you planning to go to a shopping mall this weekend?

2. Does your hometown have a good football team?

3. Is there a train station or a bus station near your school?

4. Will you please come with me to the post office?

5. Do you usually do your homework in your bedroom?

C **Work with a partner.** Take turns asking and answering the questions in **B**.

DO YOU KNOW?

The two longest steel roller coasters in the world are in _____.
a. Dubai
b. Japan
c. the United States

Communication

Make Plans Together. Choose three fun activities. Use ones from the box or your own ideas. Then find people to do them with you. Complete the calendar. Write the activity and the name of the person you are doing it with next to the time.

go shopping	bake cookies	have a treasure hunt	hang out at the mall	see a movie
play mini golf	go bowling	go to a water park	play video games	

> Do you want to see a movie tomorrow at 5:00 p.m.?

> I'm meeting my friend Kurt then. How about at 7:00 p.m.?

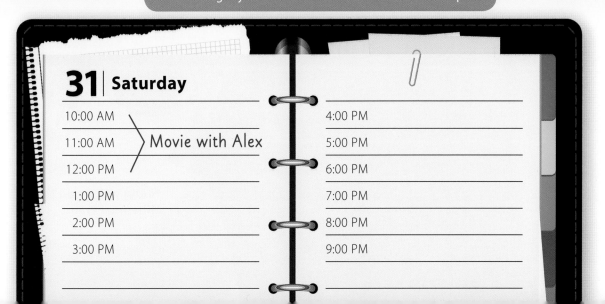

31 | Saturday

10:00 AM		4:00 PM	
11:00 AM	Movie with Alex	5:00 PM	
12:00 PM		6:00 PM	
1:00 PM		7:00 PM	
2:00 PM		8:00 PM	
3:00 PM		9:00 PM	

Reading

A **Look at the title and photo.** What do you think the Millennial Trains Project is?

B **Read the first paragraph.** Check your answer to **A**.

C **Match the person to their project.**

1. Catherine ○   ○ a. natural disasters
2. Trevor   ○   ○ b. education
3. Jenny   ○   ○ c. bookstores & libraries

Young people on the Millennial Train

THE MILLENNIAL TRAINS PROJECT

🎧 1–42

The Millennial Trains Project is a non-profit organization that enables young people to get involved in creative projects. The organization leads crowdfunded train journeys. These journeys provide young innovators with the chance to help different
5 *American communities. The organization has already completed two journeys, through the northern and central United States. Twenty-four people are now getting ready to be a part of the third.*

To earn a place on the train, each person has to raise $5,000 and have an idea for a project. At each stop, they get off the train to
10 explore a different town or city. The idea is to visit small businesses, community centers, schools—or wherever their projects take them.

Catherine Tsavalas is planning to explore how bookstores and libraries improve local communities. She wants to find out what they are doing to encourage more people to read, and what technology
15 they are using. She also wants to know if they are using social media to connect with people.

Trevor Eagle wants to make a difference to the education system. He knows that universities are becoming more and more expensive each year, and that many people think higher education is no longer
20 affordable. Over the next 10 days he is visiting seven universities. He wants to see what they are doing to meet these challenges.

Hurricanes, tornadoes, wildfires, floods—research suggests these are going to happen more and more. Jenny Gottstein thinks she can address these challenges. At each stop, she is planning to interview
25 local leaders, emergency workers, and computer game designers. She then plans to create a game to help people prepare for disasters. She believes people are more likely to remember something important when the information is fun and game-like.

These 24 people are strangers now, but not for long. The next week
30 is going to be a life-changing learning experience for many.

Comprehension

IDIOM

"It's on track"
means _____ .

a. it's happening as planned
b. it's making slow progress
c. it's come to a standstill

A Answer the questions about *The Millennial Trains Project.*

1. **Main Idea** What's another title for this article?

   a. A Train Journey with a Difference

   b. How to Crowdfund Your Next Train Journey

   c. Journey to Explore the Education System

2. **Detail** Which of these things does the second paragraph NOT mention?

   a. money raised

   b. travel time

   c. kind of places to visit

3. **Paraphrase** What is another way of saying "make a difference"? (line 17)

   a. change for the better

   b. show what's wrong and what's right

   c. completely change the system

4. **Inference** Who would probably ask, "Do you use social media to connect with users?"

   a. Catherine Tsavalas

   b. Trevor Eagle

   c. Jenny Gottstein

5. **Vocabulary** In line 24, what does the word "address" mean?

   a. talk about

   b. deal with

   c. point out

B **Complete the summary notes.** Use words from the reading.

Catherine Tsavalas

visit bookstores and
(1) _____ ; find out
what (2) _____
people are using

Trevor Eagle

visit (3) _____
universities; look at what
people are doing to meet
(4) _____

Jenny Gottstein

talk to local leaders,
(5) _____ workers,
game designers;
create a (6) _____

C **CRITICAL THINKING** **Talk with a partner.** Which project sounds the most interesting? Why? Imagine you were one of the passengers. What project would you choose?

Writing

Look back at your calendar on page 51. Write an email saying what you're doing on Saturday.

Subject: Saturday

Hi Rika,

I'm sorry but I can't meet you on Saturday. I have a really busy day. In the morning, at 10 a.m., I'm seeing a movie with my friend Alex . . .

VIDEO

World Traveler

ABOUT THE VIDEO

Kasha Slavner travels the world with a purpose.

BEFORE YOU WATCH

Circle the correct answers. What do you remember about Kasha Slavner?

Kasha is traveling around the world with her (**mom** / **sister**). She wants to see how people live in different communities and make a (**documentary** / **TV series**) and book about her experiences. Her book is going to be called (***Reflections of the Sunrise Storyteller*** / ***Global Sunrise***).

WHILE YOU WATCH

A Check your answers to the Before You Watch question.

B **Watch the video again.** Check the statements that you think Kasha might say.

"After my trip is over I want to star in a movie." ◯

"People are often disconnected with issues in foreign countries." ◯

"My main aim is to save endangered animals." ◯

"I want to use my skills in photography to help people." ◯

"When I arrive home, I think I'll have different opinions about my own community." ◯

Kasha greeting a Maasai woman in Tanzania

AFTER YOU WATCH

Talk with a partner. Do you think projects like Kasha's can help make the world a better place?

WHAT WILL EARTH BE LIKE IN THE FUTURE?

Melting ice caps in Norway

Preview

A **Use a dictionary.** Circle the words in the box that mean "become larger." Underline the words that mean "become smaller."

> fall   rise   shrink   expand   increase   decrease

B 🎧1–43 **Guess.** How do you think global warming will affect Earth? Circle to complete the sentences below. Then listen and check your answers.

1. Temperatures will (**fall** / **rise**).

2. The number of wildfires will (**increase** / **decrease**).

3. Deserts will (**shrink** / **expand**).

4. Farmland will (**shrink** / **expand**).

5. Food supplies will (**increase** / **decrease**).

C **Talk with a partner.** What do you think some other effects of global warming will be?

I think ocean levels will rise in the future.

Yeah. And I think the size of cities will . . .

Language Focus

A 🎧 1-44 **Listen and read.** Then repeat the conversation and replace the words in blue.

REAL ENGLISH   Probably

B **Practice with a partner.** Replace any words to make your own conversation.

1 Do you think temperatures will **rise** a lot in the future?

Probably. Global warming is a serious problem.

increase
go up

2 Well, when it gets hotter, **farmlands will shrink**.

How will it affect us?

deserts will expand
freshwater levels will fall

3 And what will happen when **farmlands shrink**?

Do you really want to know?

deserts expand
freshwater levels fall

4 There will be less food!

What? **Are you serious**? We should do something to stop global warming!

Are you kidding
Are you joking

🎧 1-45

MAKING PREDICTIONS ABOUT THE FUTURE

What **will** the future **be like**?	It **will be** hotter and drier.	
Will there **be** a lot more people?	Yes, there **will**. There **will** (probably) **be** a lot more people.	won't = will not
	No, there **won't**. There (probably) **won't be** a lot more people.	
Do you think food prices **will increase**?	Yes, I do. I think they**'ll increase**.	
	No, I don't. I don't think they**'ll increase**.	
There **will be more** wildfires.	There **will be more** pollution.	
There **will be fewer** animals.	There **will be less** food.	

C 🎧1-46 **Complete the information.** Use *will* and a word from the box. Listen and check.

be   disappear   hold   go   (not) be   need   rise

Global warming is very real to the people of the Maldives. Scientists think it's likely that—
sometime this century—the island nation (1) _____ because of global warming.
When ice melts, ocean levels (2) _____ . This (3) _____ a huge
problem for the country. On average, the islands are only 1.3 meters above sea level. Because
ocean levels rise about 9 millimeters per year, experts predict that many people
(4) _____ able to stay in their homes. No one knows exactly where they
(5) _____ , but they (6) _____ to find a new place to live. To attract
attention to their problem, the government recently held a meeting underwater. The
president joked that it's where they (7) _____ their meetings in the future.

D **Complete the sentences.** Use *more*, *fewer*, or *less*.

1. There will be _____ drinking water in the future.

2. There will be _____ electric car users.

3. I think there will be _____ trees in our forests.

4. In 20 years, I think there will be _____ food for people to eat.

5. I think there will be _____ environmental problems in 2050.

6. I think _____ people will travel to space.

E **Turn to page 126.** You are going to take a survey to see if you are an optimist
or a pessimist.

**Government
officials held an
underwater meeting
in the Maldives.**

The Real World

Six Degrees

Mark Lynas is a National Geographic Emerging Explorer. In his book, *Six Degrees,* Lynas predicts what changes global warming will bring to the Earth. He describes what will happen when temperatures increase by six degrees.

A 🎧1–47 **Predict.** What do you think will happen when Earth's temperature increases 1°C, 2°C, or 3°C? Discuss with a partner. Then listen to the interview and check your guesses.

1°C ⚪   ⚪ a. The Amazon rain forest might burn down.

2°C ⚪   ⚪ b. Freshwater supplies will decrease.

3°C ⚪   ⚪ c. Most coral reefs will disappear.

B 🎧1–48 **Listen to the rest of the interview.** Check (✓) the things Lynas says we can do to reduce or adapt to global warming.

◯ Decrease our use of oil and natural gas.   ◯ Decrease our use of nuclear power.

◯ Use more wind and solar energy.   ◯ Grow more genetically modified crops.

Discussion. Small day-to-day things, like recycling, can help stop global warming. Can you think of more examples? Which do you do?

Pronunciation

Reduction: *will*

A 🎧 1-49 **Listen and repeat.** Notice how *will* is reduced after pronouns.

    a. I'll   b. you'll   c. he'll   d. she'll   e. we'll   f. they'll

B 🎧 1-50 **Listen.** Write the words you hear.

1. _____ find ways to reduce pollution.

2. _____ try to reduce my carbon footprint.

3. _____ find a way to stop global warming.

4. I believe _____ run out of oil and gas in the next 100 years.

C **Work with a partner.** Take turns to read the sentences in **B**.

Communication

Make predictions. Work in a group. Choose a topic and a time. Predict what will happen in the future. Then see if your group members agree or disagree.

TOPIC	TIME
the environment	in the next year or two
exploration	in five years
technology	in the next 10 to 20 years
transportation	by 2040
education	within 50 years
medicine	in my lifetime
entertainment	sometime this century
energy	in 500 years
pollution	sometime in the future

A man flying with a jetpack

In five years, I think people will fly to work.

I don't think that will happen in five years. But it'll probably happen in my lifetime.

Reading

A **Look at the title and photo.** What do you think "on thin ice" means?

    a. strong and powerful

    b. in a bad situation

    c. changing

B **Find these words and phrases in the article.** Then circle words in the text that tell you their meaning.

> cracked   ice floes   carcasses   extinct

C **Read the text.** Underline the predictions.

As ice melts in the Arctic, polar bears have to swim farther and farther to find ice floes.

ON THIN ICE

🎧 1–51

Paul Nicklen waited patiently on a sheet of ice in the Arctic. He was there to take pictures for National Geographic. Finally, he saw something big and white. It was a polar bear, swimming toward food in the icy water.

5 Nicklen lay down on the ice to get a better photo. The swimming bear jumped out of the water to catch its food. Unfortunately, the ice cracked, or broke, and the bear fell back into the water. The polar bear couldn't find a meal, and had to swim farther away to find food.

To understand the polar bear's problem, you need to know two 10 things about the Arctic. First, it's mostly ocean. Second, the Arctic Ocean is mostly covered in ice. In the winter, the ice forms a thick, white sheet, but in summer the ice is thinner, and breaks into pieces. Sea ice is the key to survival for Arctic animals. However, because of global warming, Arctic temperatures are rising and polar ice is melting.

15 Polar bears need ice to hunt seals—their favorite meal. They stand on the ice floes, or large pieces of floating ice, and wait for the seals to come up for air. As Arctic ice melts, polar bears have to swim farther to find ice floes. Sometimes, bears have to swim more than 200 kilometers to find an ice floe. Some bears cannot swim that far 20 and, sadly, they drown.

On his last trip, Nicklen saw three polar bear carcasses. Before global warming threatened Arctic ice, a dead bear was a rare sight. Nicklen was sad to see the dead bodies. Wildlife experts think that global warming will have a terrible effect on polar bears. In the future, polar 25 ice will continue to shrink and endanger the bears. Some scientists believe that 65 percent of the world's polar bears will disappear by 2050. In other words, polar bears are in danger of becoming extinct.

Comprehension

A **Answer the questions about *On Thin Ice*.**

1. `Main Idea` What is the main idea of the article?

   a. Polar bears are amazing swimmers.

   b. Arctic temperatures are rising.

   c. Global warming is endangering polar bears.

2. `Inference` Why was the polar bear that Nicklen saw swimming unlucky?

   a. It fell in the water.

   b. It was on an ice floe.

   c. It had to swim farther.

3. `Detail` How do polar bears hunt seals?

   a. They wait on ice floes.

   b. They wait in the water.

   c. They drown the seals.

4. `Vocabulary` In line 22, "a rare sight" means something that _____.

   a. is horrible to look at

   b. you don't see often

   c. is blind

5. `Inference` Polar bears _____.

   a. won't have any food in 2050

   b. will all die before 2050

   c. are struggling to find food

IDIOM

An activity that helps strangers feel relaxed together is _____.

a. a snow melter
b. a frost cracker
c. an ice breaker

B **Complete the flow chart.** Write the effects of global warming in the correct places.

a. Some polar bears drown.

b. Polar ice melts.

c. Temperatures rise.

d. Polar bears are in danger of becoming extinct.

e. Polar bears have to swim farther between ice floes.

f. Ice breaks into ice floes.

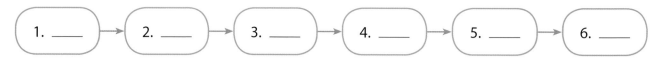

1. _____ 2. _____ 3. _____ 4. _____ 5. _____ 6. _____

C **CRITICAL THINKING** **Talk with a partner.** What other animals are being affected by global warming? Can you think of any ways to help?

Writing

Write a short paragraph. Predict what your town, city, or country will be like in the future.

My city will be very different in the future. It's a popular place to live now, and I think more and more people will move into the city. This will make apartments and houses more expensive. I think there will be more subway lines in the future...

Polar Ice

ABOUT THE VIDEO

Ice glaciers in Antarctica are melting faster than ever before.

BEFORE YOU WATCH

Quiz. What do you know about Antarctica? Circle the correct answer.

1. You can find the (**North** / **South**) Pole in Antarctica.

2. Antarctica is (**bigger** / **smaller**) than Europe.

3. (**90** / **60**) percent of all the ice on Earth is in Antarctica.

WHILE YOU WATCH

A Check your answers to the Before You Watch questions.

B **Watch the video again.** According to the video, which of these will probably happen if Antarctica's glaciers melt? Check (✓) the correct answers.

- ◯ seas will be colder
- ◯ many animals will lose their homes
- ◯ sea levels will rise
- ◯ cities and towns near the sea will disappear
- ◯ there will be more rain

AFTER YOU WATCH

Talk with a partner. What other places in the world do you think global warming will affect? Discuss.

A ship carves a path through ice floes.

WHEN DID IT
HAPPEN?

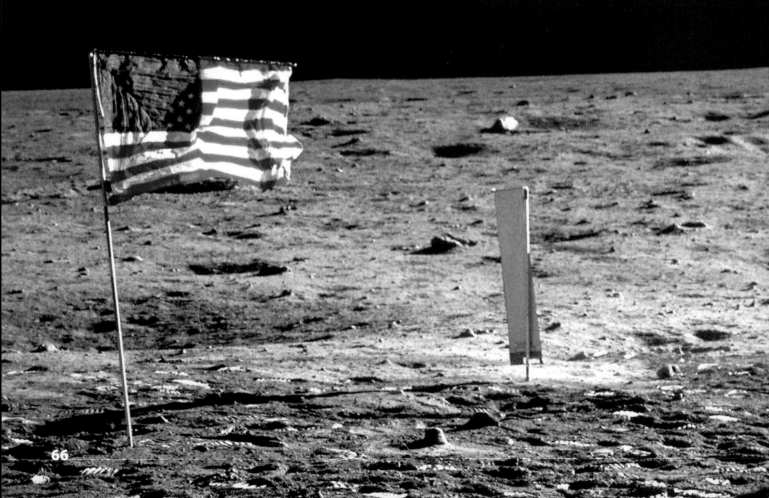

Preview

A 🎧2-01 **Listen.** Match each person with his or her achievement.

1. Co-founded Apple. (in _____)   ○   ○ a. Taylor Swift

2. Walked on the moon. (in _____)   ○   ○ b. Steve Jobs

3. Finished writing the first Harry Potter book. (in _____) ○   ○ c. Robert Ballard

4. Discovered *Titanic*. (in _____)   ○   ○ d. J. K. Rowling

5. Sold a million copies of her album *Red*   ○   ○ e. Buzz Aldrin
   in one week. (in _____)

B 🎧2-01 **Listen again.** Write the correct year next to the achievement in **A**.

C **Match.** What categories do the facts in **A** belong to? Write 1–5 below. Take turns saying trivia about each topic.

Technology _____   *Entertainment* _____   *History* _____   *Art & Literature* _____

> Steve Jobs died in 2011.

> Tablets first became popular about five years ago.

**Astronaut Buzz Aldrin
on the moon**

Language Focus

A 🎧2–02 **Listen and read.** Then repeat the conversation and replace the words in blue.

REAL ENGLISH What a . . . !

B **Practice with a partner.** Replace any words to make your own conversation.

1 Hey, Nadine, is this you in the picture?

Yeah. That's me as a baby. My hair was **a mess**!

so messy
such a mess

2 This was **around 2005**. Look at my hair! What a disaster!

Um. I think it looks fine.

in the mid 2000s
about ten years ago

3 **When did you go to New York?**

Two years ago. My hair is terrible in that photo, too!

When did you visit
When were you in

4 You know, **your hairstyle never changes**.

What? That's not true!

you have the same hairstyle now
your hair looks just the same now

🎧 2–03

TALKING ABOUT HISTORICAL EVENTS	
Point in time	
When was the first World Cup?	It was **in** 1930.
How long ago did the Chinese invent fireworks?	They invented them about 800 years **ago**.
When did the first space walk take place?	It took place **on** March 18, 1965.
Period of time	
How long was *Titanic* lost for?	It was lost **for** 73 years.
When did cell phones become popular?	They first became popular **in** the 1990s.
When did Leonardo da Vinci live?	He lived **from** 1452 **to** 1519.

C 🎧2-04 **Complete the conversation with the correct words.** Then listen and check your answers.

Zoe: You're a fan of the *Star Wars* movies, right?

Eric: I'm a *huge* fan. Why?

Zoe: When did the first one come out?

Eric: It was (1) _____ 1977. Actually, I can tell you the exact date. It came out (2) _____ May 25, 1977.

Zoe: How do you know that? That's about 40 years (3) _____!

Eric: I told you—I'm a huge fan. It was so big at the time. There were a lot of science fiction movies (4) _____ the late 1970s because of *Star Wars*.

Zoe: And when did the next two movies come out?

Eric: *The Empire Strikes Back* came out (5) _____ 1980 and *Return of the Jedi* came out (6) _____ 1983. But then there was a long gap until the next one. Fans had to wait (7) _____ 16 years until *The Phantom Menace*. There were no movies (8) _____ 1983 (9) _____ 1998.

Zoe: And we now have three new movies! You must be so excited!

D **Work with a partner.** Unscramble the words to make questions. Can you guess the answers? (You will find out the answers later in the unit.)

1. the Great Depression / how long / last / did   _____?

2. did / when / disappear / Amelia Earhart   _____?

3. when / jazz / popular / did / first / become   _____?

4. were / together / the Beatles / how long   _____?

5. take place / the first moonwalk / did / when   _____?

E **In your notebook, create a timeline like the one below.** Add 10 important events from your life to the timeline. Then share your timelines in a group.

Born   got a bike   Now

In 2008, I got my first cell phone.

How long ago did you get your second cell phone?

Hidden Depths

Robert Ballard is a National Geographic Explorer. As a boy, he liked to read about shipwrecks. He read a lot about *Titanic*. His lifelong dream was to find this great ship. On August 31, 1985, Ballard's dream came true. He found the wreck of *Titanic* four kilometers (2.4 miles) under the sea.

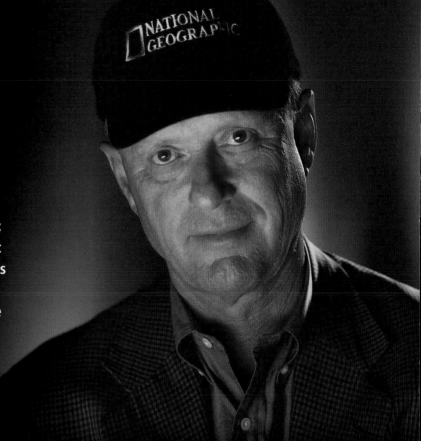

A 🎧2–05 **Listen.** Match the date to the discovery.

1. 1985 ○   ○ a. *Yorktown*
2. 1989 ○   ○ b. *Titanic*
3. 1998 ○   ○ c. *Bismarck*

B 🎧2–06 **Listen.** Circle the correct answer.

1. When *Titanic* sank, it was traveling to (**Southampton, England** / **New York, U.S.A.**).

2. Ballard first studied *Titanic* (**with a robot** / **by going inside**).

3. In 1986, Ballard reached the ship in a (**small submarine** / **a big deep-sea vehicle**).

4. Ballard wants to (**protect** / **move**) the ship.

Titanic **was found in the North Atlantic Ocean.**

CRITICAL THINKING   Robert Ballard thinks no one should take things from *Titanic*. Many explorers, however, think they should be moved to a safer place. Who do you agree with?

Pronunciation
Syllable stress

A 🎧2-07 **Listen and repeat.** Notice how the syllable stress sometimes changes when the form of a word changes.

1. de<u>fine</u>   de<u>fi</u>nition
2. <u>o</u>rigin   o<u>ri</u>ginal
3. ex<u>plore</u>   explo<u>ra</u>tion
4. com<u>pose</u>   compo<u>si</u>tion

B 🎧2-08 **Listen.** Underline the stressed syllable in each word.

1. invite   invitation
2. combine   combination
3. educate   education
4. modify   modification
5. simplify   simplicity
6. supervise   supervision

C **Work with a partner.** Take turns to read the words in **B**.

Communication

Play a trivia game. Work in a group of three. **Student A:** Go to page 127.
Student B: Go to page 128. **Student C:** Go to page 130.

Spain's players celebrate winning the 2010 World Cup final in Johannesburg, South Africa.

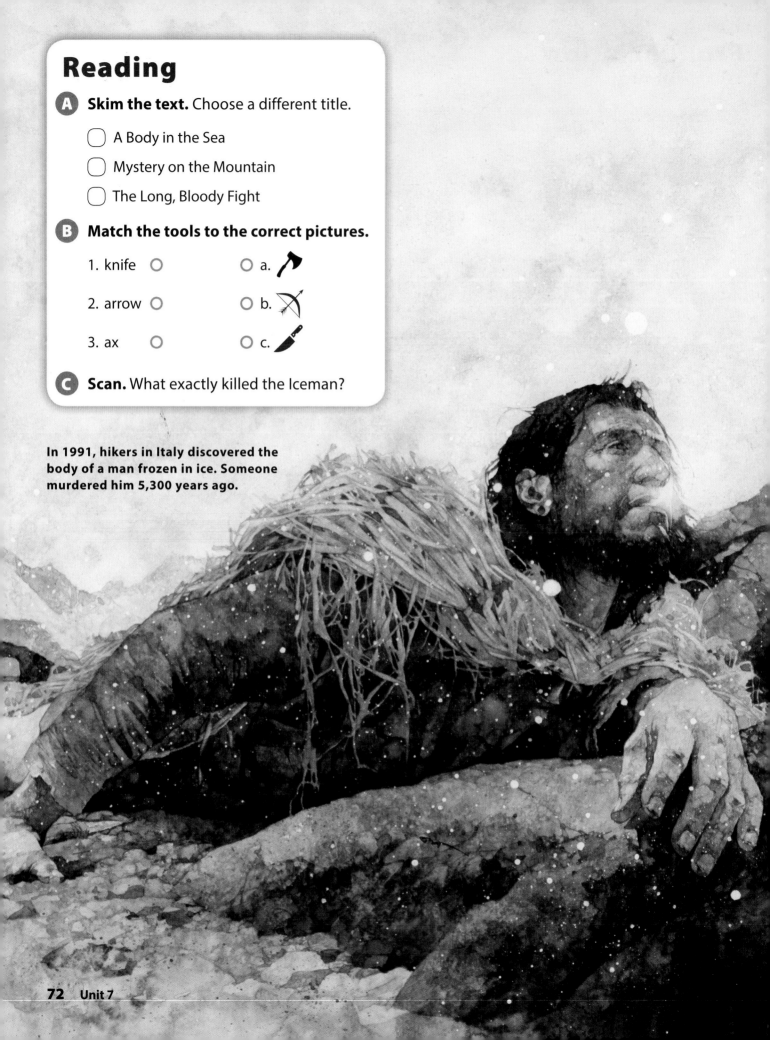

Reading

A **Skim the text.** Choose a different title.

- ○ A Body in the Sea
- ○ Mystery on the Mountain
- ○ The Long, Bloody Fight

B **Match the tools to the correct pictures.**

1. knife ○   ○ a.
2. arrow ○   ○ b.
3. ax ○   ○ c.

C **Scan.** What exactly killed the Iceman?

In 1991, hikers in Italy discovered the body of a man frozen in ice. Someone murdered him 5,300 years ago.

AN ANCIENT MURDER

🎧 2–09

In 1991, hikers in the Italian Alps found the body of a man frozen in ice. The hikers assumed that the frozen remains belonged to a mountain climber. The rescuers were shocked to discover that, rather than being a modern-day mountain climber, the man died about
5 5,300 years ago!

Scientists tried to find out more about the Iceman's life. By studying him closely, they found that he wore layers of clothing. His shoes were made of bearskin. He carried a stone knife and wooden arrows. He also had a copper ax—considered a very valuable tool thousands
10 of years ago. This tells us he was probably a rich man. He had a fire-starting kit, so we know he could make fire. Studies of his teeth and skull show he was not young. He was probably in his mid-forties.

Scientists also found wounds on the Iceman's body, showing that he died a violent death. But how exactly did he die? Scientists found a
15 piece from a stone arrow in his left shoulder. They believe this is what killed him. They also found blood on his clothes and wounds on his hands. Studies of the hand wounds show they were already beginning to close. It's unlikely that he got the injuries in a fight with his attackers. They happened much earlier.

20 In 2009, scientists studied the Iceman again. This time, they found bread and goat meat in his stomach. This means that he ate a big meal just before his death. They believe he was probably resting when he died, and someone attacked him from behind. The most likely theory today is that the Iceman got into a fight and ran up into
25 the mountains. He then had a meal, and was resting at the time of his murder. Scientists still don't know why his attackers killed him.

Will we need to rewrite the story of the Iceman again? Perhaps. Scientists continue to study history's oldest murder mystery. New technology may provide more clues about his life and death.

Comprehension

A **Answer the questions about *An Ancient Murder*.**

1. Purpose What is the purpose of the second paragraph?

   a. to show that the Iceman was a typical man of his time

   b. to explain how scientists understand so much about the Iceman

   c. to explain why the Iceman was carrying a copper ax

2. Reference In line 15, what does "this" refer to?

   a. his left shoulder

   b. a piece of stone

   c. a violent death

3. Cause and Effect Where did the wounds on the Iceman's hands come from?

   a. an earlier fight

   b. a fight with his murderer

   c. an accident with his knife

4. Detail What did scientists find in 2009 that changed their thoughts about the Iceman?

   a. blood on his clothes

   b. wounds on his hands

   c. food in his stomach

5. Detail What DON'T scientists know about the Iceman?

   a. his age

   b. what he ate

   c. who killed him

IDIOM

You say "the rest is history" when _____ .

a. everyone knows the rest of the story

b. the rest of the story is not important

B **Add the events to the timeline.** Write the letters.

a. The Iceman was resting.

b. The Iceman died.

c. The Iceman became frozen in ice.

d. The Iceman ate a large meal.

e. The Iceman got cuts on his hands from a fight.

f. The Iceman ran into the mountains.

g. Someone attacked the Iceman with an arrow.

C **CRITICAL THINKING** Talk with a partner. Why do you think the Iceman was killed? Was it for his possessions? Can you think of any other explanations for his death?

Writing

Write a blog post about someone you admire.

Home   BLOG   Photos   Contact   About Me

Serena Williams is a tennis player who is also a fashion designer, actress, and voice artist. She was born on September 26, 1981, in the United States. She is one of the most successful tennis players of all time. Serena became the world number one for the first time in . . .

Cleopatra

ABOUT THE VIDEO

Cleopatra was a successful queen who ruled her country for over two decades.

BEFORE YOU WATCH

Guess. What do you know about Cleopatra? Circle the correct answers.

Cleopatra was 1. (**a Roman** / **an Egyptian**) queen who lived around 2. (**1,000** / **2,000**) years ago. She became queen when she was 3. (**18** / **30**) years old. She married a Roman named 4. (**Marc Antony** / **Julius Caesar**). Together they were very powerful, but their relationship ended when they 5. (**got divorced** / **died**) in 30 B.C.

WHILE YOU WATCH

A Check your answers to the Before You Watch question.

B **Watch the video again.** Number the events of Cleopatra's life (1–8) in the order they happened.

__1__ Cleopatra became Queen of Egypt.

____ Cleopatra met Julius Caesar.

__5__ Cleopatra met Marc Antony.

____ Octavian started a war against Cleopatra.

____ Julius Caesar died.

____ Cleopatra got married.

____ Cleopatra's brother forced her from power.

____ Cleopatra died and so did her empire.

AFTER YOU WATCH

Talk with a partner. Can you think of another famous leader from the past? Tell their story to a partner.

Ancient carvings of Cleopatra, Dendera, Egypt

HAVE YOU EVER BEEN TO A
FESTIVAL?

Preview

A 🎧 2–10 **Listen.** Where do the speakers celebrate these events? Complete the sentences using the countries in the box below.

India	Ecuador	the U.S.	Japan	China

GIFTS

1. People in _____ celebrate the Mid-Autumn Festival. ○   ○ a. perfume

2. People in _____ celebrate Valentine's Day. ○   ○ b. mooncake

3. People in _____ celebrate White Day. ○   ○ c. flowers

4. People in _____ celebrate Quinceañera. ○   ○ d. cookies

5. People in _____ celebrate Diwali. ○   ○ e. a necklace

B 🎧 2–10 **Listen again.** What gift did each person receive? Match the gifts to the events.

C **Talk with a partner.** Ask and answer questions about giving and receiving the gifts in **A**.

> Have you ever given flowers as a gift?

> Yes, I have. Have you?

The Fire Dragon Dance is performed to celebrate the Mid-Autumn Festival.

Language Focus

A 🎧 2-11 **Listen and read.** Then repeat the conversation and replace the words in blue.

REAL ENGLISH What's going on?

B **Practice with a partner.** Replace any words to make your own conversation.

1 Hey, Nadine, have you ever gotten a pet as a gift?

Yes, I have. My parents gave me a **puppy** for my birthday two years ago.

kitten
turtle

2 What about a watch? Has anyone ever given you one?

Yeah. My **aunt** gave me one last year.

mother
father

3 Hmm. Has anyone ever **bought** you flowers or chocolates?

Let me see. . . . Yes, my parents have, for Valentine's Day.

given
sent

4 What's going on, Maya?

Well, your birthday is **next week**, and I don't know what to get you!

in 10 days
next Friday

🎧 2-12

TALKING ABOUT PAST EXPERIENCES

Have you **ever been** to a carnival?	Yes, I **have**. I**'ve been** to several. No, I **haven't**.
Has she (**ever**) **received** flowers as a gift?	Yes, she **has**. Her parents gave her some. No, she **hasn't**. She's never **gotten** flowers.
I**'ve worn** a costume several times.	Me too. / I **have**, too. Oh, really? I **haven't**.
He's **never tried** mooncakes.	Me neither. / I **haven't**, either. Oh, really? I **have**.

C Match the phrases. Then ask and answer questions with a partner.

Have you ever . . . ?

played ○	○ Spanish food	seen ○	○ carrot juice	been to ○	○ a parade
eaten ○	○ table tennis	done ○	○ fireworks	ridden ○	○ a password
gotten ○	○ an A+	drunk ○	○ volunteer work	forgotten ○	○ a horse

> Have you ever eaten Spanish food?

D 🎧 2–13 **Complete the conversations with the correct forms of the verbs.** Then listen and check your answers.

1. Marcus: (1) _____ you ever _____ (**get**) flowers for Valentine's Day?

   Erin: No, but I gave them to my mom last year. Why do you ask?

   Marcus: Well, I want to take Amy to the school dance, and I want to get her something.

   Erin: (2) _____ you _____ (**ask**) her to the dance yet?

   Marcus: Yes! I asked yesterday. She answered right away. She said yes!

2. Jing: (3) _____ you ever _____ (**be**) to a Halloween party?

   Jenny: No, but my older sister (4) _____ (**be**) to several. Why?

   Jing: A friend invited me to one next week. I don't know what to wear.

   Jenny: Wear a costume! (5) _____ you ever _____ (**wear**) one?

   Jing: Yes, I wore a costume last year. It was for the Lunar New Year. I danced in the parade!

E **Work in a group.** Take turns to write three true and three false sentences about things you've done. The others guess which ones are false. Then see who remembers the most details.

> I've ridden an elephant before.

> I think that's true. You went to Thailand last year.

Valentine's Day

On February 14 each year, people all over the world celebrate Valentine's Day. It's a day of love, affection, and friendship. People show their feelings for friends and loved ones by sending cards, flowers, and other gifts. In the United States, Valentine's Day is big, big business.

A **Valentine's Day Quiz.** Guess the correct answer.

1. Around _____ of Americans celebrate Valentine's Day.

   a. 20%   b. 60%   c. 80%

2. Americans spend a total of $_____ for Valentine's Day.

   a. 20 million   b. 1 billion   c. 20 billion

3. _____ of women buy flowers for themselves.

   a. 2%   b. 15%   c. 25%

4. Around _____ pet owners buy gifts for their pets.

   a. 90,000   b. 2 million   c. 9 million

B 🎧 2–14 **Listen.** Check your answers to **A**. Then circle **T** for True or **F** for False.

1. Women spend more money on Valentine's Day than men.   **T   F**

2. The most popular Valentine's Day gift is a card.   **T   F**

3. Pet owners spend an average of $50 on their pets.   **T   F**

4. Around 6 million Americans get engaged on Valentine's Day.   **T   F**

Discussion. Have you ever celebrated Valentine's Day? If so, how did you celebrate?

Pronunciation
Past participles

A 🎧 2-15 **Listen and repeat.**

1. taken   2. seen   3. been   4. given

B 🎧 2-16 **Listen.** Complete the sentences with the words you hear.

1. Have you ever _____ a selfie?

2. Has your teacher ever _____ you a pop quiz?

3. Have you ever _____ to a tennis match?

4. Have you ever _____ Korean food?

5. Have you ever _____ a blog post?

6. Have you ever _____ an elephant?

C **Work with a partner.** Take turns to ask and answer the questions in **B**.

DO YOU KNOW?

Who receives more Valentine cards in the U.S.?
a. children
b. wives
c. teachers

Communication

Find someone who has done these things. Add two questions. Ask questions and note the names. Then add additional information. Share your survey results with your class.

HAVE YOU EVER . . .	NAME	ADDITIONAL INFORMATION
1. eaten Mexican food?		
2. lost something expensive?		
3. been rock climbing?		
4. forgotten someone's birthday?		
5. stayed up all night?		
6. seen a famous band in concert?		
7.		
8.		

Have you ever eaten Mexican food?

Yes, I have. I ate tacos last month. They were delicious.

Reading

A **Predict.** Look at the title and photo. What do you think a "bucket list" is a list of?

   a. dangerous activities

   b. things that someone wants to do

   c. people someone admires

B **Read the text.** Underline everything that each person wants to achieve.

C **Discuss with a partner.** What's on *your* bucket list?

**Bungee jumping from
a hot air balloon**

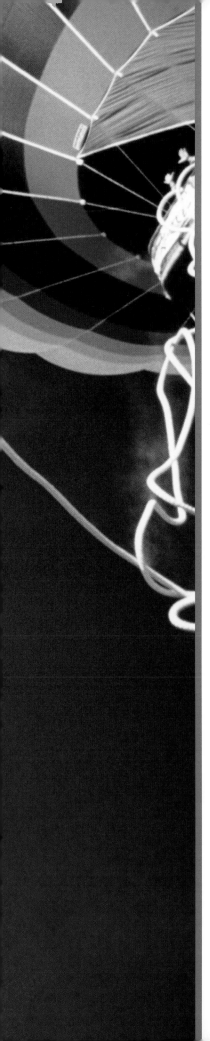

MY BUCKET LIST

🎧 2–17

Have you ever wanted to see the Great Wall of China, or win an Oscar for Best Director, or swim with dolphins? If so, you are not alone. We all have things we want to do or achieve. These are part of our "bucket lists." A bucket list is a list of things that someone wants to
5 experience in his or her lifetime. These things can be big or small. Have you ever thought about what is on your bucket list?

Lindsay Doran, 15, created her bucket list when she was 14. She has given her list serious thought. "I've always wanted to travel into space," she says. "I don't really want to be an astronaut. But I do want
10 to go to space as a tourist. I want to see the Earth from above." Other things on her list include being on TV, seeing her favorite band in concert, learning how to speak Portuguese, and living in a foreign country. "I've always wanted to live in Brazil. As part of my bucket list, I want to attend Carnaval in Rio de Janeiro," she says.

15 José Noriega, 16, recently created a list of things he wants to achieve. It changes sometimes—he adds and takes away things because he wants to keep the number of things at seven. One thing has stayed at number one, though: he wants to visit a movie set. He would like to see the *Harry Potter* or *The Hobbit* movie sets. Other things on the
20 list include being on TV, meeting his favorite sports star, living in a foreign country, skateboarding down a mountain, attending the World Cup, and backpacking across Europe. He would like to spend two months visiting Eastern Europe with his best friend Adam. "Maybe after I graduate from college," says José.

25 Carrie Kincaid, 14, also has a bucket list. She first created it when she was 12. She would like to live in a foreign country for at least two years. She also wants to learn as many foreign languages as possible. But the number one thing on her list is to see her favorite band in concert. She also wants to go on safari and to visit a movie set. Her
30 favorite movies are the *Hunger Games* and *Star Wars* series. Carrie is confident she will do most or all of the things on her bucket list. "I'm only 14," she says. "I have my whole life ahead of me!"

Comprehension

A **Answer the questions about** *My Bucket List*.

1. Main Idea People have bucket lists so that they can ____ .

   a. work toward achieving all the things they want to do

   b. tell people about the things they want to do

   c. tell people about the things that they have already done

2. Detail Why does Lindsay want to travel to space?

   a. to see Earth from above

   b. to experience what it's like to float

   c. to realize her dream of being an astronaut

3. Vocabulary In line 16, what can we replace "takes away" with?

   a. changes

   b. removes

   c. moves around

4. Detail Who was the first one to create a bucket list?

   a. Lindsay

   b. José

   c. Carrie

5. Inference Who is probably the most interested in languages?

   a. Lindsay

   b. José

   c. Carrie

> **IDIOM**
>
> If you "let your hair down," you ____ .
>
> a. relax and have a good time
> b. don't show any emotions

B **Complete the diagram.** Write the letters.

a. be on TV

b. go on safari

c. learn a foreign language

d. live in a foreign country

e. travel to space

f. visit a movie set

C **CRITICAL THINKING** **Talk with a partner.** Whose bucket list in the article do you think is most like yours? What do you think the idiom "to kick the bucket" means?

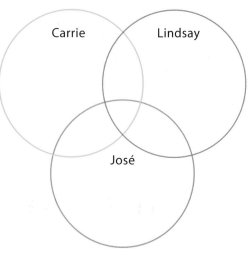

Carrie   Lindsay

José

Writing

Think of seven things you want to achieve in your lifetime. Then email your bucket list to a friend.

Subject: Bucket list

Hi Stacey,

Here's a bucket list of things I want to do in my lifetime. At number one is to see an orangutan. I've seen an orangutan on TV, but I think it would be amazing to be close to them in the wild. There are other things I want to do someday. I want to go to Paris, learn how to surf, climb a mountain, see the Northern Lights, and ride on a camel in the desert. Another thing I'd really like to do is read all of Jane Austen's . . . .

Land of Adventure

ABOUT THE VIDEO

New Zealand is home to many exciting adventure activities.

BEFORE YOU WATCH

Match. Write the correct letters (a–e) under the pictures.

> a. jet boating   b. bungee jumping   c. rafting
> d. surfing   e. hot air ballooning

1. _____ 2. _____ 3. _____ 4. _____ 5. _____

WHILE YOU WATCH

A Check your answers to the Before You Watch question.

B **Watch the video again.** Read the following statements. According to the video, which adventure sports should these people try?

1. "I want to see beautiful scenery." _____

2. "I like working in a team." _____

3. "I love speed." _____

AFTER YOU WATCH

Talk with a partner. Have you ever done an adventure sport? What adventure sports would you like to try?

PHONES
USED TO BE MUCH
BIGGER.

Preview

A 🎧2–18 **Listen.** Three people are discussing communication. Complete the sentences using the words from the box.

> write letters   sends texts   sends emails   calls   use social media   chat online

REASON

1. Paul used to _____ . Now he _____ . ○ ○ a. It's friendlier.

2. Amy used to _____ . Now she _____ . ○ ○ b. It's fast and easy.

3. Kate used to _____ . Now she _____ . ○ ○ c. It's more private.

B 🎧2–18 **Listen again.** Match the person to the reason for their preference.

C **Talk with a partner.** How do you communicate now? How did you use to communicate?

> I used to make a lot of phone calls, but now I video chat.

> I used to email a lot. Now I prefer texting.

A man talking on an early car phone

Language Focus

A 🎧2–19 **Listen and read.** Then repeat the conversation and replace the words in blue.

REAL ENGLISH for one thing

B **Practice with a partner.** Replace any words to make your own conversation.

1

Is that a new phone?

Yeah. This model used to cost a lot, but now **it's not so expensive**.

it's a lot cheaper
the price is pretty reasonable

2

I already like this much better than my old phone.

Why?

Why is that?
How come?

3

Well, for one thing, **it's a lot lighter**.

Hey, why don't you call me so I have your number?

OK.

it's much thinner
the design is better

4

What's wrong?

Um, **I don't know how to make a call!**

I'm not sure how to phone someone
I have no idea how to make a call

🎧2–20

DESCRIBING PAST HABITS

When I was a child, I **used to play** video games for hours. Cell phones **used to be** heavy, but they aren't anymore.	
My mother **didn't use to like** video-chatting, but now she loves it. In the past, I **never used to buy** clothes online. Now I do all the time.	
Did you **use to have** a desktop computer?	Yes, I did. / No, I didn't.

C 🎧 2-21 **Complete the conversations with the correct form of *used to* and the verbs given.** Then listen and check your answers.

1. Susan: Look at these old records. Are they yours?

   Paulo: No, they're my father's. He has a huge collection. He (1) _____ (**buy**) them all the time.

   Susan: Does he still play them?

   Paula: No, he (2) _____ (**play**) them after dinner sometimes, but not anymore. We don't even have a record player now.

2. Terry: (3) _____ your older sister _____ (**live**) in Montreal?

   Caitlin: Actually, she still lives there.

   Terry: Oh yeah? Do you talk to her much?

   Caitlin: Sure. I (4) _____ (**never / like**) video chatting, but now I love it. When we lived in the same town, we (5) _____ (**talk**) maybe once a week. Now we talk every couple of days!

D **Write sentences about places and things in your life that are different from before.** Discuss the changes with a partner. Which changes are good? Which are bad?

1. <u>There used to be a bookstore near my house but now there's an electronics shop</u> .

2. _____ .

3. _____ .

4. _____ .

5. _____ .

6. _____ .

E **Work with a partner. Student A:** Turn to page 128. **Student B:** Turn to page 130. You are going to compare two pictures of someone.

Apple iMacs were first introduced in 1998.

Humans and Machines

Amber Case is a National Geographic Explorer. She's an anthropologist interested in learning about the relationship between humans and technology. She wants to understand what effects technology has on our culture and society.

A 🎧 2–22 **Listen.** Circle **T** for True or **F** for False.

1. Case studies the relationship between humans and machines.   T   F

2. According to Case, a cell phone is an example of a physical tool.   T   F

3. Case wants to find out more about the importance of technology in our lives.   T   F

4. A "digital dark age" is the term used to refer to a time before technology existed.   T   F

B 🎧 2–22 **Listen again.** According to Case, technology is helping us _____. Check (✓) the things she mentions.

☐ choose the career of our choice   ☐ access information at any given time

☐ keep our worktime separate from playtime   ☐ store a lot of data for future generations

Discussion. Look at the statements in **B**. Do you agree with them? Why or why not?

Pronunciation
Reduction: *used to*

A 🎧2–23 **Listen and repeat.** Notice how *used to* and *use to* are pronounced.

1. I used to have a desktop computer, but I don't anymore.

2. I didn't use to like texting, but now I do it all the time.

B 🎧2–24 **Listen.** Complete the sentences with the words you hear.

1. Tablets _____ very expensive.

2. People _____ on their cell phones in restaurants.

3. TV programs _____ more entertaining.

4. Social media _____ popular with older adults.

5. Students _____ their textbooks online.

C **Work with a partner.** Take turns to read the sentences in **B**. Do you agree with them?

Cell phones used to weigh 1 kilogram and took 10 hours to charge.
a. True
b. False

Communication

A **Guess who wrote it.** On three pieces of paper, write three different things about yourself that used to be true. These could be surprising or embarrassing. Then mix them up and put them in a pile.

> I used to have a collection of stuffed snakes.

> I used to listen to Justin Bieber and dance around in my room.

> As a kid I used to practice walking like a fashion model in front of my mirror.

B **Take three pieces of paper and walk around the class.** Ask questions to find the person who wrote each sentence. Ask follow-up questions to get more information.

> Did you use to have a cat named Sparkle?

> No, I didn't. Did you use to wear an ugly pink headband?

Feliks Zemdegs won the World Rubik's Cube Championship in 2013.

Reading

A **Read the title and look at the pictures.** What do you think the article is about?

B **Read the first paragraph.** Underline the meaning of "fad."

C **Discuss.** Work with a partner. What are some fads you have heard of?

WHAT MAKES A FAD?

🎧 2–25

Hula hoops. Pet rocks. Tamagotchis. These things used to be very popular. Did you ever own any of these? If you didn't, don't feel too bad. They were all *fads*. A *fad* is something that becomes very popular among a large number of people, but only for a short time.
5 Something can become a fad very quickly, but can stop being popular just as quickly. When it is no longer "cool," a fad goes away. Anything can become a fad—fashion, food, entertainment, technology, even language.

In the late 1970s, a Hungarian professor of architecture named Erno
10 Rubik was looking for a creative way to teach his students about 3D objects. He invented a six-color plastic object that would be called the Rubik's Cube. The objective was to get each side of the cube a different color. It was very challenging. It took a few years for the toy to become popular, but then suddenly, in 1982, it seemed everyone
15 had one. Consumers bought over a hundred million of the toys. There were 50 books available that year offering solutions. Then, just as suddenly as the craze started, it ended. By 1983, people were not interested in the Rubik's Cube anymore, perhaps because so many people already had one in their home.

20 In 2012, a South Korean musician named Psy released a song called "Gangnam Style." The music video shows Psy pretending to horse-ride while he is dancing. In six months, it became the first YouTube video ever to reach a billion views. Six months after that, it went on to reach two billion views. The song and video started a worldwide dance
25 craze, similar to the "Macarena" dance fad from the 1990s. "Gangnam Style" had a huge influence on world popular culture. U.S. President Barack Obama and U.K. Prime Minister David Cameron even tried out the dance. Although "Gangnam Style" faded in popularity, the "Korean Wave" of culture remains popular all over the world.

Psy performing live on stage. More than 2 billion people have seen his video "Gangnam Style."

Comprehension

A Answer the questions about *What Makes a Fad?*

1. Purpose   What is the purpose of the first paragraph?

   a. to give examples of fads

   b. to explain what a fad is

   c. to show how fads become popular

2. Detail   A fad stops being a fad when _____.

   a. it becomes very popular

   b. older people start to like it

   c. people don't think it's cool

3. Cause and Effect   According to the article, people stopped buying the Rubik's Cube in 1983 because _____.

   a. it was very difficult to solve

   b. books gave away the secrets to solving it

   c. so many people already had one

> **IDIOM**
>
> Another way to say something is very popular is to say it's "_____."
>
> a. up
> b. in
> c. on

4. Inference   What helped "Gangnam Style" become such a huge worldwide hit?

   a. the Internet

   b. television

   c. the radio

5. Vocabulary   In line 28, what does "faded in popularity" mean?

   a. became less popular

   b. continued to be popular

   c. became a fad

B Complete the notes.

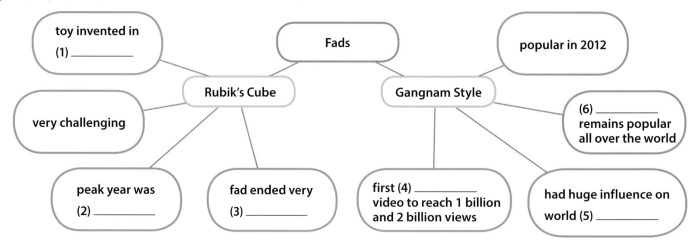

toy invented in (1) _____

very challenging

Rubik's Cube

peak year was (2) _____

fad ended very (3) _____

Fads

Gangnam Style

popular in 2012

(6) _____ remains popular all over the world

first (4) _____ video to reach 1 billion and 2 billion views

had huge influence on world (5) _____

C **CRITICAL THINKING**   Why do you think fads start and end so quickly? Can you think of any other fads?

Writing

Write a short paragraph about your favorite fad.

The *Angry Birds* game was very popular a few years ago. I downloaded the app and used to play the game for hours. Some of my friends even played the game during their classes. I remember people also used to buy . . .

Changing Times

ABOUT THE VIDEO

National Geographic Explorer Hannah Reyes explores some remote areas of the Philippines, where life is slowly starting to change.

BEFORE YOU WATCH

Guess. What do you know about the Philippines? Circle the correct answers.

1. The Philippines is a country in (**Southeast / North**) Asia.

2. There are around (**700 / 7,000**) islands in the Philippines.

3. The population of the Philippines is around (**10 / 100**) million.

4. The capital of the Philippines is (**Manila / Hanoi**).

WHILE YOU WATCH

A **Check your answers to the Before You Watch questions.**

B **Watch the video again.** Complete these sentences using words from the video.

1. People used to wear very simple clothes, but now they can buy _____ .

2. There never used to be any _____ , but now people come here to get traditional tattoos.

3. Life used to be simple, but now people have more _____ .

4. People used to _____ , but now some work in factories.

Teenage girls sing at a public school, Luzon, the Philippines

AFTER YOU WATCH

Talk with a partner. What other places do you know that have changed a lot? Describe the changes to your partner.

THEY'VE FOUND A FOSSIL.

Preview

A 🎧 2–26 **Listen to the news.** Number the pictures in the order you hear them (1–4).

 _____ footprints

 _____ mummy

 _____ skeleton

 _____ fossil

B 🎧 2–26 **Listen again.** Match the places with the statements.

1. The Sahara ◯   ◯ a. Researchers have found the skeleton of a **giant dinosaur**.

2. Germany ◯   ◯ b. Archeologists have discovered the footprints of an **early human**.

3. Kenya ◯   ◯ c. Scientists have identified the mummy of a **pharaoh**.

4. Egypt ◯   ◯ d. An explorer has unearthed the fossil of a **huge crocodile**.

C **Work with a partner.** Look at the **bold** words in **B**. Do you know what they are? Which story in **B** are you most interested in?

An explorer studies fossil remains, Utah, U.S.A.

Language Focus

A 🎧 2-27 **Listen and read.** Then repeat the conversation and replace the words in blue.

REAL ENGLISH Anyway . . .

B **Practice with a partner.** Replace any words to make your own conversation.

1 Have you been to the natural history museum recently?

No, I haven't been there **since last May**. Why?

for a long time
since I went for a class trip

2 There's a new dinosaur exhibit there. **I've been twice** and I've learned a lot.

Oh, like what?

I've seen it twice
I've been there two times

3 Well, they have a dinosaur called a Stegosaurus. It's **really interesting**.

A Stigosaurus? You mean there's a dinosaur named after me?

fascinating
pretty cool

4 No, Stig! It's a *Stego*saurus. Anyway, its brain was only the size of **a walnut**!

brain

Oh, that's not what I imagined!

an egg
a golfball

🎧 2-28

DESCRIBING PAST ACTIONS

A man **found** dinosaur bones in his yard in 1997. He **has recently taken** them to a local museum.

Workers in Mexico **came across** two human footprints several years ago. **In the past few years**, scientists **have found** 11 more footprints in the area.

In 2011, a boy **discovered** the body of a mammoth in Siberia. A museum **has displayed** the mammoth **for several years** / **since 2012**.

for
two weeks / several days / a year / a long time

since
2011 / last year / the 1990s / I was a kid

C Complete the sentences. Write *for* or *since*.

1. I've been part of the fossil research team _____ three months.

2. Jason hasn't written any research articles _____ he became a professor.

3. Penny has been a member of the Science Club _____ two years.

4. The museum has had the skeleton on display _____ 1998.

5. Archeologists have known about the footprints in the cave _____ six months.

6. Researchers haven't discovered any fossils in the area _____ last year.

D 🎧 2–29 **Complete the conversations with the correct forms of the verbs.** Then listen and check your answers.

1. Quinn: (1) _____ you _____ (*watch*) the news last night?

   Michael: No, why?

   Quinn: There (2) _____ (*be*) a cool story about fossils. In the past few weeks, some schoolchildren (3) _____ (*find*) some interesting-looking rocks. They (4) _____ (*give*) them to some scientists. It turns out they were dinosaur fossils! The scientists (5) _____ (*not come across*) anything else since then, but they are still looking.

2. Jake: Hi, sorry I'm late. How long (6) _____ you _____ (*be*) here?

   Fumiko: It's OK. I just got here two minutes ago. So, what movie do you want to see?

   Jake: How about that one? It's about aliens who come to Earth and live as humans.

   Fumiko: Um, you know, in the past few months I (7) _____ (*see*) three science fiction movies. Can we watch something else?

   Jake: I (8) _____ (*see*) the other movies last week. Let's try somewhere else.

E **Work with a partner. Student A:** Turn to page 129. **Student B:** Turn to page 131. Ask and answer questions to complete the missing information.

A meteorite falling over Whitby, England

Digging for Answers

Paul Sereno is a National Geographic Explorer. Right at this moment he may be studying, talking about, or even looking for dinosaurs. He's probably the most well-known dinosaur hunter among schoolchildren in the United States.

A 🎧2–30 **Listen.** Write the year each dinosaur was discovered in the notes below.

B 🎧2–30 **Listen again.** Complete the notes.

Eoraptor discovered in _____ ,
- found in (1) _____
- 1st dinosaurs to walk the Earth
- (2) _____ million years ago

Nigersaurus discovered in _____ ,
- found in (5) _____ Desert
- named after Niger
- size of an (6) _____

Sarcosuchus discovered in _____ ,
- found in Sahara Desert
- also known as (3) _____
- largest (4) _____ (12 meters)
- 110 million years ago

Rajasaurus discovered in _____
- found in (7) _____
- 1st dinosaur skull found in Indian subcontinent
- (8) _____ -eating

Discussion. Which of Sereno's discoveries do you think is the most interesting? Why? Imagine you discovered a new dinosaur fossil near your home. What would you name it?

Pronunciation

Reduction: *has* and *have*

A 🎧2-31 **Listen and repeat.** Notice how *has* and *have* are sometimes reduced.

1. A boy has made an amazing discovery.

2. What has he discovered?

3. The scientists have identified the fossils.

4. Why have they identified them as birds and not dinosaurs?

B 🎧2-32 **Listen.** Write the verbs you hear.

1. In the past few months, scientists _____ some interesting rocks in the area.

2. Our teacher _____ us a lot about dinosaurs.

3. Why _____ the scientists _____ their discovery a secret?

4. Some farmers _____ an old burial site on their land.

5. Where _____ Kevin _____ to do his fieldwork?

C **Work with a partner.** Take turns to read the sentences in **B**.

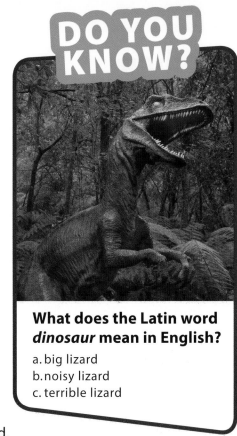

DO YOU KNOW?

What does the Latin word *dinosaur* mean in English?

a. big lizard
b. noisy lizard
c. terrible lizard

Communication

A **Hold a news conference.** Complete one of these headlines, or make up your own. Prepare to give a short news conference to report the details of your story. Organize your idea by taking notes below.

Frightened Campers See _____ in Forest

Girl Finds _____ in Backyard

Students Discover Teacher is a(n) _____

Scientists Come Across Frozen _____

| **Who** is the story about? | **What** happened? | **Where** did it happen? |
| **When** did it happen? | **Why** is the event important? | **How** does this story affect people? |

B **Take turns reporting your stories.** The rest of the students are journalists. Answer any questions they ask.

> A girl recently found a fossil of a strange creature in her backyard.

> The girl was digging a hole in her sandbox when she found the fossil. She took it . . .

Reading

A **Discuss.** Look at the title. What do you think it means?

B **Skim the text.** Choose a different title.

   a. Dinosaur Hunters

   b. Tyler Lyson's Discoveries

   c. Dinosaurs and the Movies

C **Read the text.** Underline words that describe body parts.

A model dinosaur being carried on a car in New York, U.S.A.

DINOSAURS ALIVE!

🎧 2–33

In all of the *Jurassic Park* movies, from *Jurassic Park* (1993) to *Jurassic World* (2015), dinosaurs are the stars of the show. The way the dinosaurs look, move, and roar is amazing—they seem so real! But dinosaurs haven't lived on our planet for the last 65 million years.
5 So how do filmmakers bring them to life? They ask paleontologists— or fossil experts—for help.

Paleontologist Tyler Lyson has been interested in dinosaurs since he was a child. He grew up in the countryside in the western United States, and found his first dinosaur bone when he was only six years
10 old. Lyson says the best way to learn about dinosaurs is to look at fossils. Fossils and footprints help scientists understand how dinosaurs looked, moved, and lived. There are fossils of bones and teeth in rocks, lava, and ice.

Filmmakers use fossils and other research from paleontologists to
15 build dinosaurs for their movies. But they have to use their imaginations, too. When paleontologists discover a fossil, the animal's skin and flesh have usually disappeared. The dinosaur builders have to ask lots of questions. What color was the dinosaur's skin? Did it use to have stripes or other patterns on its body? Did it
20 use to have feathers? How long was its tail?

To bring dinosaurs to life, dinosaur builders make a skeleton out of metal. Then they put a fake skin over the frame. After they have finished, the dinosaur can turn, move, and even roar! The builders scan pictures of these robot dinosaurs into a computer, and then use
25 CGI (computer-generated imagery) to animate them. Filmmakers have used CGI for all the dinosaurs in the *Jurassic Park* movies.

Paleontologists still have a lot of questions about dinosaurs. What did they sound like? How did they hunt? What did they eat? The answers to these questions will help filmmakers create even more
30 realistic dinosaurs than ever before.

Comprehension

A Answer the questions about *Dinosaurs Alive!*

1. `Detail` Which statement is NOT true about fossils?

    a. Fossils can tell us how dinosaurs lived.

    b. Scientists can find fossils in ice.

    c. Filmmakers dig for different types of fossils.

2. `Reference` In line 5, what does "them" refer to?

    a. fossils   b. dinosaurs   c. robots

3. `Main Idea` What is the main idea of the third paragraph?

    a. Filmmakers use research and their imaginations.

    b. Fossils aren't always complete.

    c. Paleontologists don't know what color dinosaurs were.

4. `Vocabulary` What is another word for "animate"? (line 25)

    a. move   b. use   c. scan

5. `Detail` What do scientists NOT know for certain about dinosaurs?

    a. how big they were

    b. when they lived on Earth

    c. how they hunted

B Complete the definitions.

| expert   paleontologist   stripe   tissue   roar |

1. A(n) _____ studies fossils and dinosaur bones.

2. A(n) _____ knows a subject very well.

3. A(n) _____ is a kind of pattern.

4. When animals _____ they make a lot of noise.

5. The material that forms parts of a plant or animal is called _____.

C CRITICAL THINKING
Talk with a partner. Do you think the dinosaurs in movies look realistic? What else have animators used CGI for?

Writing

Write a news story on a topic of your choice.

• THE DAILY NEWS •

BEAR SEEN AT PINE LAKE

There have been several bear sightings in the Pine Lake area the past few weeks. The most recent was around 10:30 last night. Campers Joel Gary and Kevin Pratt reported a bear outside their tent at Pine Lake Campground. . . .

Dinosaurs!

ABOUT THE VIDEO

Scientists find out more about the lives of dinosaurs.

BEFORE YOU WATCH

Guess. Match the two parts to make correct sentences.

1. Dinosaurs first appeared on Earth ○ ○ a. 200,000 years ago.

2. Humans first appeared on Earth ○ ○ b. 65 million years ago.

3. Dinosaurs disappeared around ○ ○ c. 225 million years ago.

WHILE YOU WATCH

A **Check your answers to the Before You Watch questions.**

B **Watch the video again.** Circle **T** for True or **F** for False.

1. The smallest dinosaurs were less than one meter long. **T** **F**

2. The smallest dinosaurs were called Sauropods. **T** **F**

3. Some modern-day animals are similar to dinosaurs. **T** **F**

4. Most scientists think dinosaurs died from a disease. **T** **F**

AFTER YOU WATCH

Talk with a partner. What's your favorite dinosaur? What do you know about it?

Dinosaurs during the Jurassic Period

11

BUY ONE, GET ONE FREE!

Customers line up
for a sale in Paris

Preview

A 🎧 2–34 **Listen to four advertisements.** What product is each advertisement selling? Number the pictures 1–4. One is extra.

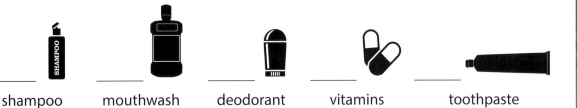

shampoo   mouthwash   deodorant   vitamins   toothpaste

B 🎧 2–34 **Listen again.** What does each advertisement say about the product?

1. If you buy one, you will (**only pay 50%** / **get one free**).

2. If you visit the website, you can (**ask for a free sample** / **see videos of the product**).

3. If you use it every day, your hair will be (**stronger** / **straighter**).

4. If you use it, it will (**kill bacteria** / **reduce tooth decay**).

C **Talk with a partner.** Which kind of advertising do you like most or like least? Why?

> I like ads on TV. Sometimes they're really funny.

> Really? I think they're a little annoying in the middle of a show.

Language Focus

A 🎧 2–35 **Listen and read.** Then repeat the conversation and replace the words in blue.

REAL ENGLISH   What a bargain!

B **Practice with a partner.** Replace any words to make your own conversation.

1 Shampoo & Conditioners

Have you ever **tried** this shampoo before?

No. I've never even heard of it.

bought
used

2 It says your hair will be **much shinier** if you use it for just one week.

I don't know . . .

stronger
more manageable

3 It also says if you buy one bottle, you'll get another one free!

What a bargain! I'm going to get it.

That's a good offer
What a great deal

4 So how do you like your new shampoo?

Um . . . I think I'll **stick to** my old brand . . .

go back to
continue to use

🎧 2–36

TALKING ABOUT RESULTS

If you **use** this shampoo, your hair **will be** shinier.

If you **use** this shampoo, you **won't need** conditioner.

You **can save** money **if** you **buy** two.

If you **don't buy** this today, you'll regret it.

If you **don't buy** it today, you **won't be able to buy** it later.

If I **buy** three, **will** I **get** a discount?

  Yes, you **will**. / No, you **won't**.

What **will** you **do if** the store **is** closed?

  I'll **go** to another store.

C Match the two parts to complete the sentences.

1. If you read the ad carefully, ○   ○ a. you won't see any ads.

2. If you turn on the ad blocker, ○   ○ b. you can find some great deals.

3. If you fill in this survey, ○   ○ c. we'll enter your name in the prize draw.

4. If you shop in different stores, ○   ○ d. you'll see it makes a lot of claims.

D 🎧 2-37 **Unscramble the sentences.** Add commas if necessary. Listen and check.

(1) _____.

(*will want to listen to this / you / like to sing / if / you*). Introducing the shower microphone! It's a sponge to keep you clean, *and* a microphone to help you practice your singing.

(2) _____.

(*if / will keep you busy for hours / you / this / like to have fun*). Sing as loudly as you like—and keep clean doing it! The cost? Only $9.95.

(3) _____.

(*there / and if / call in the next five minutes / won't be any shipping or handling charges / you*). That's right! Shipping and handling will be free! But wait! There's more.

(4) _____.

(*will include an extra shower microphone / you / we / call right now / if*). That's two for the price of one! But hurry! Supplies are limited. We're waiting for your call.

E **Work in a group.** Think of three goals. Use the ideas below or your own ideas. Other group members, say one thing you think will happen if the speaker achieves each goal.

save more money	study English more	get a part-time job	exercise more
do volunteer work	eat less junk food	quit social media	watch TV less

I'd like to exercise more.

If you do that, you'll feel a lot healthier.

The Real World

Why We Buy

Paco Underhill is an expert on shopping habits. He is the author of the book *Why We Buy*. Over the past 20 years, he has spent thousands of hours watching people shop. He talks about simple things that stores can do to increase their sales.

A 🎧 2–38 **Listen.** What advice do you hear? Circle the correct answer.

1. Don't open a store near a (**restaurant** / **bank**).

2. A store should never place new items for sale near the (**entrance** / **cash register**).

3. A store should place new products to the (**left** / **right**) of the entrance.

4. Stores should put (**baskets** / **items on sale**) in the back of the store.

5. If you put (**chairs** / **new electronics**) in a store, people will be able to shop longer.

B 🎧 2–38 **Listen again.** Complete the sentences.

1. Bank windows are _____ , so people start walking fast when they see a bank.

2. If you place items near the front door, people will tend to _____ them.

3. Shoppers tend to _____ and _____ toward the right when they enter a store.

4. If people pick up baskets when their hands are full, they'll _____ .

5. Shopping partners usually need a place to _____ .

CRITICAL THINKING   Do you have any ideas to help a store improve its sales?

Pronunciation

Pausing in *if* clauses

A 🎧 2-39 **Listen and repeat.** Notice the pause after the comma when an *if* clause begins the sentence.

If you use this shampoo, your hair will be shinier.

Your hair will be shinier if you use this shampoo.

B 🎧 2-40 **Listen to the sentences.** Which ones have a pause in the middle? Write **P** (Pause) or **NP** (No Pause).

1. _____   2. _____   3. _____   4. _____   5. _____   6. _____

C **Work with a partner.** Take turns to read the sentences on page 108.

DO YOU KNOW?

In an ad, the small bit of toothpaste on a toothbrush is called a _____ .

a. pea
b. nurdle
c. blobby

Communication

Create a TV commercial. Work with a partner. Choose one of the products given below or think of your own. Prepare the script for a short TV commercial. Consider the questions below and take notes. Then present your commercials.

> chocolate-flavored toothpaste   heated tennis shoes   breath mints for pets

What makes the product interesting?	How will you explain its interesting features?
How much does it cost?	Will viewers get anything extra if they order right away?

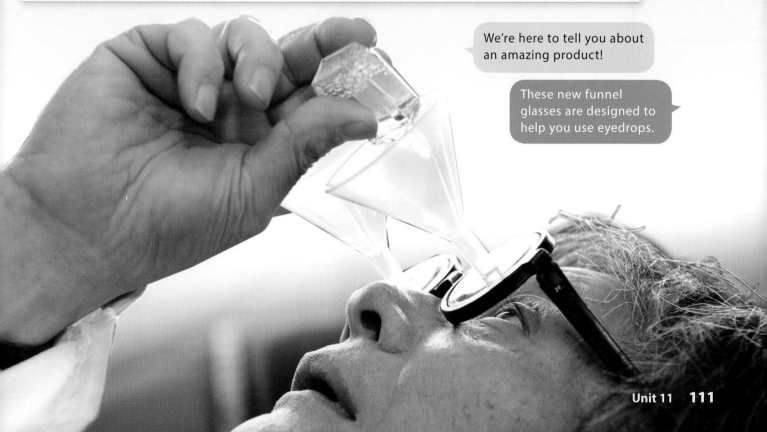

We're here to tell you about an amazing product!

These new funnel glasses are designed to help you use eyedrops.

Reading

A **Look at the title.** "Cause Marketing" refers to the partnership between _____ .

   a. two businesses   b. two charities   c. a business and a charity

B **Skim the reading.** Match the campaigns to their descriptions.

   1. Eatiply   ○   ○ a. Reverse marketing in action

   2. Don't Buy This   ○   ○ b. Do a good deed for a total stranger

   3. Pay It Forward   ○   ○ c. Have a meal and help others

C **Read the text.** Underline the benefits of cause marketing.

Customers drink coffees in Naples, Italy. The tradition of buying two and leaving one gave rise to the Pay It Forward campaign.

CAUSE MARKETING

🎧 2–41

You've probably heard of marketing, but have you ever heard of cause marketing? This usually refers to a partnership between a business and a charity. Instead of simply trying to sell more products and make more money, cause marketing also aims to do some good.
5 Here are examples of some recent cause marketing campaigns.

Eatiply Eatiply is a "hunger project" with a simple concept: If you eat a meal, a needy person will eat for free. Restaurants that are part of the Eatiply project have certain dishes or special meals they want to promote. If you order one of these dishes, the restaurant will donate
10 a meal to someone in need. Often, this person might be homeless—probably living in the same city. This means that the customer doesn't really need to do anything special or pay any more money. Just by ordering a certain dish, you can help out someone in need.

Don't Buy This How often have you heard a company tell you *not* to
15 buy its products? Yet that's exactly what a U.S. company did in 2013. Patagonia—a maker of outdoor clothing—launched an advertising campaign telling people *not* to buy their products. Instead, the company promised certain things: If you bring your torn or ripped clothing to them, they'll repair it. If you give them your old clothes,
20 they'll find a way to pass them on to other people, or to recycle them. The message is simple—we are all consuming too much, and need to find ways to reduce, reuse, and recycle.

Pay It Forward The phrase "pay it forward" refers to the act of repaying a good deed to a new person. Many companies have
25 picked up on this idea and launched "pay it forward" campaigns. For example, if you go to buy a coffee, you might choose to pay for two coffees. If a needy person then comes into the coffee shop, they'll get a free coffee. The people who buy the first coffee usually never meet the recipients, but still feel they've done a good deed.

30 Many companies believe that customers respond better to cause marketing campaigns. It gives people the chance to do some good while shopping or eating, but it also creates good publicity and goodwill for the companies that participate.

Comprehension

A **Answer the questions about *Cause Marketing*.**

1. Main Idea The main aim of "Cause Marketing" is to ____.

   a. help a cause   b. promote a charity   c. recycle products

2. Detail In the Eatiply scheme, if you want to help a needy person you need to ____.

   a. pay extra money

   b. order a special dish or meal

   c. sign up for the project

3. Inference The Patagonia clothing company's campaign implies their products ____.

   a. are made from recycled material

   b. last longer and can be repaired

   c. are expensive because they're environmentally-friendly

4. Inference In the Pay It Forward campaign, who pays for the free coffee?

   a. a customer

   b. the coffee shop

   c. the charity

5. Vocabulary What does "goodwill" mean? (line 33)

   a. a positive attitude

   b. a good business environment

   c. good profits

B **Complete the summary notes.** Use words from the reading.

Eatiply	Patagonia	Pay It (6) _____
free (1) _____ for a person in (2) _____ when a customer buys a certain dish or meal	an outdoor (3) _____ company that encourages its customers to (4) _____ , (5) _____ , and recycle	customers can (7) _____ for an extra coffee or meal when they buy their own, the company donates this to a needy person; it encourages people to do a good (8) _____

C **CRITICAL THINKING** **Talk with a partner.** Do you think companies also benefit from cause marketing? Why or why not? Do you have any ideas for a cause marketing campaign?

Writing

Write about your idea for a new marketing campaign.

I have a good idea for a new marketing campaign using my phone. Companies could advertise on people's phone cases. They could pay me to have their company name or logo on my phone case. Then all my friends and family would see it and learn more about the company. I think this would help . . .

Supermarket Tricks

ABOUT THE VIDEO

Supermarkets use special tricks to make people spend more money.

BEFORE YOU WATCH

Match. Write the words in the box under the pictures.

> shopping cart   checkout   customer   receipt

_____

_____

_____

_____

WHILE YOU WATCH

A **Check your answers to the Before You Watch question.**

B **Watch the video again.** Complete these sentences using words from the video.

1. If customers are _____, they will stay longer and buy more.

2. If the shopping cart isn't _____, people will put more in it.

3. If customers take their _____, they will ask for presents.

4. If they put candy near the _____, people will pick it up while they're waiting to pay.

A child looks at candy in a supermarket, California, U.S.A.

AFTER YOU WATCH

Talk with a partner. What supermarket do you usually go to? Have you ever noticed the tricks you saw in the video?

WHICH IS THE BIGGEST PLANET?

sun

1   2   3   4

planets

Preview

A 🎧 2–42 **Listen.** A teacher is helping students remember the planets. Write the sentence she teaches them. Then match the planets with the numbers.

_____

_____ Mars   _____ Mercury   _____ Neptune   _____ Earth

_____ Uranus   _____ Saturn   _____ Jupiter   _____ Venus

B 🎧 2–43 **Listen.** Complete the summary with words from the picture.

Our (1) _____ is called the Milky Way. The (2) _____ is one of many (3) _____ in the Milky Way. Eight (4) _____ move around the sun. These, together with the sun, make up our (5) _____ .

C **Talk with a partner.** Take turns asking and answering questions about our solar system.

> Which planet is between Mercury and Earth?

> It's Venus. Which planet has rings?

5

6

7

8

planets

galaxy

stars

Language Focus

A 🎧 2–44 **Listen and read.** Then repeat the conversation and replace the words in blue.

REAL ENGLISH I have no idea.

B **Practice with a partner.** Replace any words to make your own conversation.

🎧 2–45

USING DIFFERENT TENSES

Present Tenses	**Future Tenses**
Astronauts **go** to the space station several times a year.	The rocket **takes off** in 15 minutes.
A crew of three astronauts **is waiting** to take off.	They**'re staying** on the space station for the next six days.
	All of them **are going to travel** into space for the first time.
Past Tenses	
They **felt** uncomfortable while they **were training**.	Soon they**'ll have** a great view of Earth.
Present Perfect	**Conditional Clauses**
They**'ve trained** for this trip for two years.	**If** they **cancel** this launch, they**'ll go** next month.

C 🎧 2–46 **Complete the conversation by circling words.** Then listen and check.

Chris: What (1) (**do you do** / **are you doing**)?

Beth: (2) (**I give** / **I'm giving**) a presentation next week, so (3) (**I'm researching** / **I used to research**) my topic.

Chris: Oh, yeah? What (4) (**are you planning** / **did you use to plan**) to talk about?

Beth: (5) (**I've talked** / **I'm going to talk**) about the spacecraft Voyager 1.
(6) (**I used to be** / **I've been**) interested in space ever since I was in elementary school. My third-grade teacher (7) (**taught** / **has taught**) us about it.

Chris: (8) (**I don't know** / **I'm not going to know**) anything about it.

Beth: Well, NASA (9) (**launched** / **was launching**) Voyager 1 in 1977. From 1977 to 2012, it (10) (**traveled** / **has traveled**) through our solar system. It carried all kinds of things from Earth, like recordings of languages, music, and photos. If aliens (11) (**find** / **will find**) this spacecraft, (12) (**they learn** / **they'll learn**) a lot about Earth. Well, (13) (**they learn** / **they'll learn**) about Earth in 1977.

Chris: What (14) (**happened** / **has happened**) in 2012?

Beth: (15) (**It left** / **It's going to leave**) our solar system. Since then it (16) (**was continuing** / **has continued**) to travel. But scientists think (17) (**it runs out of** / **it'll run out of**) power around 2025.

D 🎧 2–47 **Complete the sentences.** Use the correct form of words. Listen and check.

In 1969, the spacecraft Apollo 11 (1) _____ (*land*) on the moon for the first time. Since then, scientists (2) _____ (*learn*) many things about our closest neighbor. Only 12 people (3) _____ (*be ever*) to the moon. Those astronauts (4) _____ (*go*) there between 1969 and 1972. This was during a period of time when scientists (5) _____ (*study*) the moon very closely.

Today, NASA astronauts (6) _____ (*plan*) another trip to the moon. They (7) _____ (*want*) to go before 2020. If they (8) _____ (*go*), they (9) _____ (*learn*) more about the moon than ever before. Other countries (10) _____ (*make*) preparations to go to the moon, too. India, China, Japan, and Russia all (11) _____ (*have*) plans in place. Some private companies (12) _____ (*hope*) to make a profit from moon tourism. They (13) _____ (*begin*) to take reservations for future flights.

E **Work in pairs. Student A:** Turn to page 127. **Student B:** Turn to page 131. You are going to see how much you know about space.

Space Inventions

Many of the inventions we use every day come from technology NASA first developed for use in space. For example, technology in NASA's space boots was so good that shoe companies quickly adapted it for sneakers on Earth.

A **Look at the inventions below.** Here are some products that use space technology. What problems do you think their technology solved in space? Discuss with a partner. Then listen and check your answers.

> water filters   coated eyeglass lenses   ear thermometers

B **Listen again.** Circle **T** for True or **F** for False.

1. Some companies use NASA's water filtering technology to make water bottles.   T   F

2. Infrared thermometers measure a person's temperature from inside their mouth.   T   F

3. The new thermometers can measure temperature in two seconds.   T   F

4. The problem with plastic glasses is that they break easily.   T   F

5. Coating eyeglasses with thin plastic makes them scratch-proof.   T   F

Discussion. Which of the inventions in **A** do you think is the most useful? Why? Do you know any other technologies developed by NASA?

Pronunciation
Linking of /w/ and /y/ sounds

A 🎧 2–49 **Listen and repeat.** Notice the /w/ and /y/ sounds between some words.

1. Your movements are slow in space.
   /w/

2. Pluto is not a planet anymore.
   /w/

3. Mercury and Venus are closer to the sun than Earth.
   /y/

4. The astronauts have to be at the launchpad by 7:00.
   /y/

B 🎧 2–50 **Listen to the sentences.** Circle the places you hear /w/ or /y/ sounds.

1. The spacecraft finally entered Earth's atmosphere.

2. You can see over 2,000 stars at night.

3. Scientists didn't know about Pluto until 1931.

4. In 1969, two Americans landed on the moon in Apollo 11.

5. Do you think there will be a space colony on the moon someday?

6. Astronauts have to do a lot of training before they can go into space.

C **Work with a partner.** Take turns to read the sentences in **B**.

Communication

Make a group decision. Work in a small group. Imagine your spacecraft has to make an emergency landing on the moon. You will live there for one month. The space station has food and water. As a group, choose eight things to take with you.

a pen	paper	a game console	magazines	a knife	your favorite movie
a mirror	sunglasses	a laptop	a camera	a soccer ball	your favorite book
a radio	a telescope	a deck of cards	your music collection	_____	_____

We'll need something to read. Why don't we take some magazines?

That sounds good. And let's take a game console.

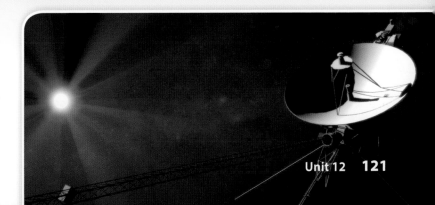

Reading

A **Scan.** Underline the year in which a spacecraft first landed on a comet.

B **Look at the headings.** Match the detail to the correct heading. Then scan and check your predictions.

1. Rosetta would fly for 10 years.   ○   ○ The Mission

2. Organic materials exist on comets. ○   ○ The Landing

3. Philae bounced twice on the comet. ○   ○ The Findings

C **Read the passage.** Find answers to the two questions in the first paragraph.

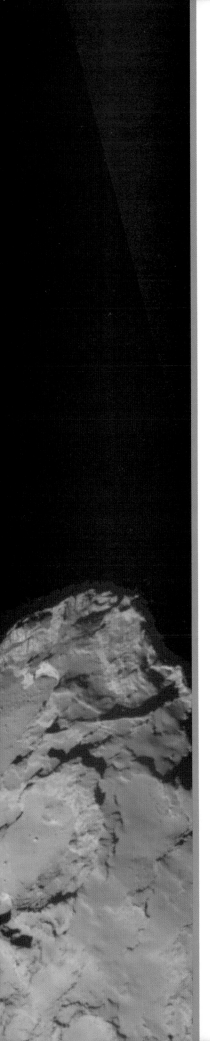

LANDING
on a COMET

🎧 2–51

On November 12, 2014, scientists from the European Space Agency (ESA) made history by successfully landing a spacecraft on a comet. This marked the end of a 10-year, 6.5-billion-kilometer journey. How did they achieve this feat? Why was the mission important?

5 The Mission
There are billions of comets in our solar system. But until the 1980s, everything we knew about them came from looking through telescopes. In 1986, scientists sent several spacecraft to fly by and study Halley's Comet. These returned valuable data, but scientists
10 needed another mission to answer further questions. In 1993, the ESA began planning another mission to a comet called 67P. The new spacecraft would not just fly by the four-kilometer-long comet—it would land on it. In 2004, the ESA launched Rosetta into space. After ten years and billions of kilometers, Rosetta reached the comet in
15 August 2014, and began its orbit from a distance of 30 kilometers.

The Landing
On board Rosetta was Philae, a washing machine-sized lander. On November 12, Philae separated from Rosetta and approached the comet. After landing, Philae bounced twice before stopping seven
20 hours later. Philae began to send data to the orbiting Rosetta, which then sent the data back to Earth. Some scientists say the most difficult part of the mission was the touchdown—the comet was traveling at 130,000 kilometers an hour, and had an uneven shape.

The Findings
25 The first photos sent back to Earth showed that Philae was in the shadow of a cliff. This was not ideal, as the lander depends on sunlight to recharge its battery. But Philae managed to gather a huge amount of data—data that will keep scientists busy for a long time. Scientists learned, for example, that the comet's surface is much harder than
30 expected, and that some organic materials exist on comets. What scientists learn could also help us understand where Earth's oceans came from. It's possible that a comet brought water to Earth billions of years ago. This could even help explain the origin of life on Earth.

Comprehension

A Answer the questions about *Landing on a Comet*.

1. Vocabulary What does the word "feat" mean? (line 4)

   a. an achievement

   b. a mission

   c. a historical event

2. Inference Scientists needed another mission to a comet because the first mission _____ .

   a. didn't return useful data

   b. raised more questions

   c. wasn't able to collect any data

3. Inference If the lander's battery runs out of power, Rosetta will _____ .

   a. have to land on 67P

   b. replace the battery

   c. stop receiving data from Philae

4. Detail According to the article, which part of the mission was the hardest?

   a. the journey to 67P

   b. the landing on 67P

   c. analyzing the results from Rosetta

5. Detail Scientists believe that the comet's data may help explain the origins of _____ .

   a. our solar system

   b. life on Earth

   c. the Milky Way

> **IDIOM**
>
> When you are "over the moon," you are _____ .
>
> a. serious
> b. lost
> c. very happy

B Complete the timeline. Use information from the passage.

1986

2004

1993
ESA plans mission

2014
Philae lands on 67P

pre 1980s

C Talk with a partner. Do you think life may exist on other planets? What other space missions do you know about?

Writing

Write your own personal statement saying what you think about the Rosetta mission.

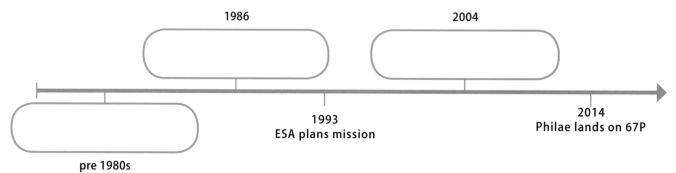

My name is Park Hee-jin. I have been interested in space and other planets since I was a little girl. In fact, I used to play a game called "space" with my friends, and we would always pretend to live on Jupiter! I think the Rosetta mission is amazing and will help scientists discover more about life on Earth and space. I hope the data will prove that there may be life on other planets . . .

Mission to Mars

BEFORE YOU WATCH

Guess. How did the Curiosity rover land on Mars? Number the pictures (1–4) in the order you think they happened.

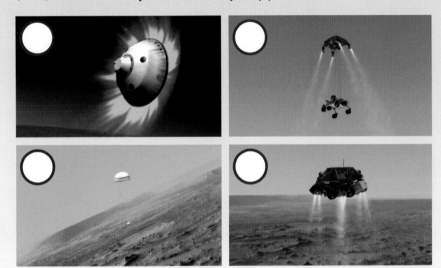

WHILE YOU WATCH

A **Check your answers to the Before You Watch question.**

B **Watch the video again.** Circle the correct answer.

1. Curiosity has been on Mars for (**less / more**) than 2 years.

2. Curiosity is the same size as a small (**dog / car**).

3. It took Curiosity (**9 months / 9 years**) to travel to Mars.

4. The most difficult part of the mission was (**landing on Mars / entering the atmosphere**).

AFTER YOU WATCH

Talk with a partner. Which planet in the solar system would you most like to visit? What would you want to find out about that planet?

The Curiosity rover on the surface of Mars

UNIT 1 COMMUNICATION

Student A: Look the picture below. The girls' names are missing. Ask your partner questions to complete the names.

Wendy   Tina   Beth   Grace   Delia

Student A

Sam   Josh   Tom   Kevin   Ricardo

Which one is Wendy?

She's the one who is sitting on the couch.

Is she the one who's reading a book?

UNIT 6 LANGUAGE FOCUS

Ⓐ Take a survey. Take turns asking and answering these questions with a partner. Mark your and your partner's responses.

1 = Yes, definitely   2 = Yes, probably   3 = No, probably not   4 = No, definitely not

50 YEARS FROM NOW, DO YOU THINK . . . ?	YOU	YOUR PARTNER
1. people will live longer		
2. everyone will have enough food		
3. scientists will find a cure for cancer		
4. global warming will be stopped		
5. there will be less pollution		
6. food will become cheaper		
7. new types of energy will become common		
8. the world will be a better place for everyone		

Ⓑ Add up your numbers. The lower the number, the more optimistic you are about the future; the higher the number, the more pessimistic you are.

UNIT 7 COMMUNICATION

Student A: Take turns asking questions and giving the three possible answers. Check (✓) the questions the other two students get correct. (The correct answers are in **bold**.)

			Student B	Student C
1. When did disco music first become popular?			◯	◯
a. in the 1950s	b. **in the 1970s**	c. in the 1990s		
2. How long were the Beatles together?			◯	◯
a. **for 10 years**	b. for 20 years	c. for 30 years		
3. When did the nun Mother Teresa live?			◯	◯
a. from 1860 to 1945	b. from 1880 to 1976	c. **from 1910 to 1997**		
4. When did Spain last win the World Cup?			◯	◯
a. in 2008	b. **in 2010**	c. in 2014		
5. When did the United States become independent?			◯	◯
a. on October 12, 1492	b. on January 1,1608	c. **on July 4, 1776**		

UNIT 12 LANGUAGE FOCUS

Student A: Take turns asking questions and giving the three possible answers. Check (✓) the questions the other student gets correct. (The correct answers are in **bold**.)

			Student B
1. After the moon, what's the brightest object in the night sky?			◯
a. **Venus**	b. Mars	c. Jupiter	
2. What is the moon slowly doing?			◯
a. moving toward Earth	b. **moving away from Earth**	c. getting larger	
3. In 1981, what did NASA add to space missions?			◯
a. donuts	b. **M&M candy**	c. pretzels	
4. How many people have visited the International Space Station so far?			◯
a. around 50	b. around 125	c. **around 215**	
5. If you fly a ship between Mars and Jupiter, what are you going to see?			◯
a. Halley's Comet	b. **lots of asteroids**	c. a moon shared by both	

UNIT 7 COMMUNICATION

Student B: Take turns asking questions and giving the three possible answers. Check (✓) the questions the other two students get correct. (The correct answers are in **bold**.)

	Student A	Student C

1. When did Amelia Earhart disappear?
   a. in 1909   b. in 1919   c. **in 1937**   ◯   ◯

2. When was the Cold War?
   a. from 1917 to 1939   b. **from 1947 to 1991** c. from 1968 to 2012   ◯   ◯

3. What year did Michael Jackson's album *Thriller* come out?
   a. in 1970   b. **in 1982**   c. in 1998   ◯   ◯

4. When did Princess Diana live?
   a. from 1926 to 1962   b. from 1940 to 1975   c. from **1961 to 1997**   ◯   ◯

5. How long ago did the Finns invent ice skates?
   a. **5,000 years ago**   b. 3,000 years ago   c. 1,000 years ago   ◯   ◯

UNIT 9 LANGUAGE FOCUS

A **Student A: Look at this picture of Rick from ten years ago.** Your partner has a picture of Rick today. Ask and answer questions to find out what's different. Find at least five differences.

Rick used to have long hair. Does he still have long hair?

No, now he has short hair. Did he use to have a tablet?

UNIT 1 COMMUNICATION

Student B: Look the picture below. The boys' names are missing. Ask your partner questions to complete the names.

Sam   Ricardo   Kevin   Josh   Tom

Which one is Josh?

He's the one who is standing in front of the painting.

UNIT 10 LANGUAGE FOCUS

Student A: You and Student B have the same information, but some parts are missing. Ask and answer questions to complete the missing information.

Dawn Tyson has lived (1) _____ (**where?**) for over 50 years. Dawn has had a quiet life. She got married (2) _____ (**when?**). She has worked at the supermarket since 2002. On the night of August 4, she heard (3) _____ (**what?**) outside. She went outside to investigate. She saw a large hole in her backyard. A large reddish rock was in the hole. She called (4) _____ (**who?**). They showed the rock to some scientists. They said a meteorite landed in Dawn's yard. A meteorite is worth a lot of money. The local museum paid $75,000 for Dawn's rock.

UNIT 3 REAL WORLD

Real Signs: 1 (No dogs allowed), 2 (No campfires), 8 (No magnets)

UNIT 7 COMMUNICATION

Student C: Take turns asking questions and giving the three possible answers. Check (✓) the questions the other two students get correct. (The correct answers are in **bold**.)

		Student A	Student B
1. When did the first moonwalk take place? a. on November 22, 1963 b. **on July 20, 1969** c. on July 4, 1976		○	○
2. How long ago did the Italians invent eyeglasses? a. **700 years ago** b. 500 years ago c. 300 years ago		○	○
3. When did Apple release the first iPhone? a. in 2000 b. **in 2007** c. in 2012		○	○
4. When did jazz first become popular? a. **during the 1920s** b. during the 1950s c. during the 1980s		○	○
5. When did *The Simpsons* first air on TV? a. **in 1989** b. in 1999 c. in 2009		○	○

UNIT 9 LANGUAGE FOCUS

A **Student B: Look at this picture of Rick today.** Your partner has a picture of Rick from ten years ago. Ask and answer questions to find out what's different. Find at least five differences.

Rick used to have long hair. Does he still have long hair?

No, now he has short hair. Did he use to have a tablet?

UNIT 10 LANGUAGE FOCUS

Student B: You and Student A have the same information, but some parts are missing. Ask and answer questions to complete the missing information.

Dawn Tyson has lived in Dayton for over 50 years. Dawn has had a (1) _____ (**what kind of?**) life. She got married at age 24. She has worked (2) _____ (**where?**) since 2002. On the night of August 4, she heard a loud noise outside. She went outside to investigate. She saw (3) _____ (**what?**) in her backyard. A large reddish rock was in the hole. She called the police. They showed the rock to (4) _____ (**who?**). They said a meteorite landed in Dawn's yard. A meteorite is worth a lot of money. The local museum paid $75,000 for Dawn's rock.

UNIT 12 LANGUAGE FOCUS

Student B: Take turns asking questions and giving the three possible answers. Check (✓) the questions the other student gets correct. (The correct answers are in **bold**.)

		Student A

1. Which planet is the closest in size to Earth?
   a. Mars   b. **Venus**   c. Mercury   ◯

2. How many moons does Saturn have?
   a. 2   b. 17   c. **62**   ◯

3. What food have NASA astronauts requested in space more than any other?
   a. **shrimp cocktail**   b. steak and eggs   c. roast chicken   ◯

4. How long have there been man-made satellites in space?
   a. since the 1940s   b. **since the 1950s**   c. since the 1960s   ◯

5. What will the sun eventually become?
   a. a black hole   b. **a white dwarf**   c. a comet   ◯

UNIT 4 REAL WORLD

True Facts: Frogs can change color. Frogs never close their eyes.

IRREGULAR PAST TENSE VERBS

BASE FORM	PAST FORM	PAST PARTICIPLE
become	became	become
bring	brought	brought
buy	bought	bought
catch	caught	caught
choose	chose	chosen
come	came	come
cost	cost	cost
cut	cut	cut
draw	drew	drawn
drink	drank	drunk
drive	drove	driven
eat	ate	eaten
fall	fell	fallen
feel	felt	felt
fight	fought	fought
find	found	found
fly	flew	flown
get	got	gotten
give	gave	given
go	went	gone
grow	grew	grown
hear	heard	heard
hurt	hurt	hurt
keep	kept	kept
know	knew	known
let	let	let
lose	lost	lost

BASE FORM	PAST FORM	PAST PARTICIPLE
make	made	made
mean	meant	meant
meet	met	met
pay	paid	paid
put	put	put
read	read	read
ride	rode	ridden
run	ran	run
say	said	said
see	saw	seen
sell	sold	sold
show	showed	shown
sing	sang	sung
sleep	slept	slept
speak	spoke	spoken
steal	stole	stolen
swim	swam	swum
take	took	taken
teach	taught	taught
tell	told	told
think	thought	thought
throw	threw	thrown
understand	understood	understood
wear	wore	worn
win	won	won
write	wrote	written

LANGUAGE NOTES

UNIT 1 WHICH ONE IS JUSTIN?

WHICH ONE/ONES

Which one	are	you?	I'm	the one	in sunglasses. with short hair.
	is	your friend? Rachel?	He's She's		
Which ones	are	your friends Beth and Lara?	They're	the ones	by the window. on the couch.

RELATIVE CLAUSES (WHO)

He's the one She's the one	who	's holding a coffee. 's wearing a baseball cap. has long, dark hair.
They're the ones	who	are laughing. are standing by the door. look really bored.

Is he the one Is she the one	who	's talking to Rich?	Yes, he is. No, he isn't. Yes, she is. No, she isn't.
Are they the ones	who	are wearing shorts?	Yes, they are. No, they're not.

UNIT 2 I'D LIKE TO BE A PILOT.

WANT / WOULD LIKE

What	do you want	to be someday?	I want	to be a pilot.
	would you like		I'd like	

WORK AS / WORK WITH / WORK FOR

I'd like to	**work as**	an astronaut. a photographer. an artist.
	work with	children. animals. computers.
	work for	a small company. a multinational company. National Geographic.

LET + OBJECT PRONOUN + VERB

This job **lets**	me you him her us them	**travel**.

RELATIVE CLAUSES (*THAT*)

I want I'd like to have	a job	that	is creative. lets me work with computers.
I don't want I wouldn't like			is boring. doesn't pay well.

UNIT 3 PLEASE DON'T FEED THE MONKEYS.

BE ALLOWED TO (PERMISSION)

I am	**allowed to** **not allowed to**	use a cell phone in class. take photos in the museum. wear sneakers at school.
You are We are		

CAN (PERMISSION)

I You We	can can't	use a cell phone in class. take photos in the museum. wear sneakers at school.

HAVE TO (OBLIGATION)

I You We	have to don't have to	stay on the bike path. wear a uniform at school. go to school on Saturdays.

YES/NO QUESTIONS—SHORT ANSWERS

Are	you we	allowed to	use a cell phone in class? take photos in the museum? wear sneakers at school?	Yes, you are. No, you aren't.

Can	you we		use a cell phone in class? take photos in the museum? wear sneakers at school?	Yes, you can. No, you can't.

Do	you we	have to	stay on the bike path? wear a uniform at school? go to school on Saturdays?	Yes, you do. No, you don't.

UNIT 4 HOW DO SLOTHS MOVE?

ADVERBS OF MANNER

Sloths are **quiet**. Dogs are **quick** learners. Are owls **patient** hunters?	Sloths move **quietly**. Dogs learn **quickly**. Do owls hunt **patiently**?
Bees are **hard** workers. Rabbits are **fast** runners.	Bees work **hard**. Rabbits run **fast**.
Dolphins are **good** swimmers.	Dolphins swim **well**.
How does a tiger hunt?	It hunts **quietly** and **fiercely**.

FORMING ADVERBS FROM ADJECTIVES

Most adjectives	Add -ly	slow bad	slowly badly
Adjectives ending in -y	Drop -y Add -ily	easy happy	easily happily
Adjectives ending in -le	Drop -e Add -y	gentle terrible	gently terribly
The adjectives *early, fast, hard, late,* and *high*	No change	early hard	early hard
The adjective *good*	Change to *well*	good	well

UNIT 5 I'M MEETING FRIENDS LATER.

SIMPLE PRESENT FOR SCHEDULED FUTURE EVENTS (FIXED BY TIMETABLE)

I **have** an appointment at 10:00 tomorrow.

The train **leaves** at 6:50 p.m. tonight.

Their flight **lands** in 20 minutes.

Does tonight's movie **begin** at 8:00?	Yes, it does.
What time **do** the banks **open** tomorrow?	They **open** at 9:00.
When **does** your sister's bus **get** in?	It **gets** in on Friday morning.

PRESENT PROGRESSIVE FOR FUTURE PLANS (PREARRANGED EVENTS)

I**'m going** shopping after class.

He**'s working** on Saturday and Sunday.

They**'re having** a party on Friday night.

Are you **staying** in town this weekend?	Yes, I am.
What **are** you **doing** after class?	I**'m seeing** a movie.
Where **are** you **going** on your next vacation?	We**'re going** to Los Angeles.

UNIT 6 WHAT WILL EARTH BE LIKE IN THE FUTURE?

FUTURE WITH *WILL* (PREDICTIONS)

What **will** the future **be** like?	In the future it **will be** hotter and drier.
	We **won't have** a lot of fresh drinking water.

There		**be** more pollution.
We	**will** **won't**	**use** more nuclear power.
Deserts		**expand**.

Will there **be** more pollution?	Yes, there **will**. There **will** probably **be** a lot more pollution.
	No, there **won't**. There probably **won't be** more pollution.
Do you think there **will be** more pollution?	Yes, I **do**. I think there **will** probably **be** a lot more pollution.
	No, I **don't**. I don't think there **will be** more pollution.

CONTRACTION (*WILL*)

I **will**	I**'ll**
You **will**	You**'ll**
He **will**	He**'ll**
She **will**	She**'ll**
We **will**	We**'ll**
They **will**	They**'ll**

MORE / FEWER / LESS

More Fewer		More Less	
	trees		land
	cars		food
	roads		pollution
	deserts		fresh water
	wildfires		solar energy
	animals		freedom
	plants		rain
	natural resources		flooding
	problems		stress

UNIT 7 WHEN DID IT HAPPEN?

POINT IN TIME

Nelson Mandela became president of South Africa	**in** 1994. **on** May 10, 1994. more than 20 years **ago**.

PERIOD OF TIME

Nelson Mandela led South Africa	**from** 1994 **to** 1999. **during** the 1990s. **for** five years.

Point in time   **Period of time**

UNIT 8 HAVE YOU EVER BEEN TO A FESTIVAL?

PRESENT PERFECT (EXPERIENCES)

I You We They	**have** **haven't**	**been** to a festival.
He She	**has** **hasn't**	

Have	you they	(ever) tried mooncakes?	Yes, I **have**. / No, I **haven't**. Yes, they **have**. / No, they **haven't**.
Has	he she		Yes, he **has**. / No, he **hasn't**. Yes, she **has**. / No, she **hasn't**.

CONTRACTION (*HAVE* AND *HAS*)

I **have** You **have** We **have** They **have** He **has** She **has**	I**'ve** You**'ve** We**'ve** They**'ve** He**'s** She**'s**

(*TOO* AND *EITHER*)

I have been to Spain.	**Me too.** I have, **too**.
I haven't ridden a horse.	**Me neither.** I haven**'t**, **either**.

UNIT 9 PHONES USED TO BE MUCH BIGGER.

USED TO (DO)

I You He She We They	used to didn't use to never used to	text a lot.

Did	you he she they	use to have a laptop?	Yes, I did. / No, I didn't. Yes, he did. / No, he didn't. Yes, she did. / No, she didn't. Yes, they did. / No, they didn't.

UNIT 10 THEY'VE FOUND A FOSSIL.

PRESENT PERFECT (RECENT EVENTS)

What	has he has she	discovered?	He has She has	discovered a fossil.
	have you have they		I/We have They have	

SINCE / UNTIL NOW / IN THE LAST . . . YEARS

Scientists **have looked for** fossils in this area **since 2006**.

Since 2006, scientists **have looked for** fossils in this area.

People **have not found** many fossils in the area **until now**.

Until now, people **have not found** many fossils in the area.

Some teenagers **have come across** some unusual fossils **in the last few years**.

In the last few years, some teenagers **have come across** some unusual fossils.

RECENTLY

Recently, two girls **have discovered** a mammoth skull.

Two girls **have recently discovered** a mammoth skull.

Two girls **have discovered** a mammoth skull **recently**.

UNIT 11 BUY ONE, GET ONE FREE!

FIRST CONDITIONAL (STATEMENTS)

If	you **use** this mouthwash,	you **will be** happy with your choice. you **won't want** another brand.
	you **don't use** this mouthwash,	you **will have** bad breath. you **won't have** fresh breath.

You **will receive** a free gift You **can get** a 20% discount We **can't take** your call We **won't charge** shipping and handling	if	you **call** in the next ten minutes.
We **will accept** cash We **can take** a debit card You **can't make** the purchase You **won't receive** a discount		you **don't have** a credit card.

FIRST CONDITIONAL (QUESTIONS AND SHORT ANSWERS)

If	I we	**call** now, **will** you **include** the free gift?	Yes, we **will**. No, we **won't**.
	he she	**orders** today, **can** they **send** it right away?	Yes, they **can**. No, they **can't**.

If	I we	**call** now, what **will** you **include**?	A free gift.
	he she	**orders** today, when **can** they **send** it?	Right away.

UNIT 12 WHICH IS THE BIGGEST PLANET?

SIMPLE PRESENT (PRESENT ACTIONS)

The Earth **orbits** the sun.
The moon **doesn't have** an atmosphere.

SIMPLE PRESENT (FUTURE ACTIONS)

The rocket **takes off** in 30 minutes.
The ship **stops** at the space station tomorrow afternoon.

PRESENT PROGRESSIVE (PRESENT ACTIONS)

The astronauts **are waiting** for takeoff.

Voyager **is exploring** beyond our solar system now.

PRESENT PROGRESSIVE (FUTURE ACTIONS)

They **are starting** their training next week.

The astronauts **are giving** a presentation to some students on Friday.

FUTURE WITH *WILL*

Space tourism **will become** common in the future.

The comet landing **will give** scientists important data to study for many years.

SIMPLE PAST

The scientist William Herschel **discovered** Uranus in 1781.

The lander **touched down** on the comet in 2014.

PAST PROGRESSIVE

Apollo 13 **was traveling** to the moon when there was an accident.

NASA **was planning** to launch last Saturday but they delayed it.

USED TO

Pluto **used to be** a planet, but it's not called a planet anymore.

Scientists **used to think** Venus was like Earth.

PRESENT PERFECT

People **have looked** up at the stars for thousands of years.

I **have read** many books about space and space travel.

FIRST CONDITIONAL

If we **build** a space station on Mars, we **will learn** a lot.

Your body **can become** weak **if** you **spend** a long time in space.

Photo Credits

1 Boom Chuthai/500px Prime, **3** Laurent Bouvet/Rapsodia/Aurora Photos, **4–5** Silken Photography/Shutterstock**, 6–7** Hero Images Inc/Hero Images/Corbis, **9** Hill Street Studios/Blend Images/Alamy, **10** Max Lowe, **11** (t) Marta Iwanek/Getty Images, (b) Liushengfilm/Shutterstock, **12–13** Courtesy of Tamara Reynolds, **14** Monkey Business Images/Shutterstock, **15** Aaron Huey/NGC, **16–17** Skip Brown/NGC, **19** Minerva Studio/ Shutterstock, **20** Sean Kenney Design, **21** (t) FingerMedium/Getty Images, (b) belizar/Shutterstock, **22–23** Xinhua/eyevine/Redux, **25** Mark Thiessen/NGC, **26–27** Tiana Voogt, **28–29** (b) Paul Prescott/Shutterstock, **29** (tr) Dim Dimich/Shutterstock, **30** (t) Andy Clark/Reuters, **31** (tr) Val Thoermer/Shutterstock, **32** (c) Xpacifica/NGC, (b) Johnny Nicoloro, **33** (c) Randy Olson/NGC, (b) Raul Touzon/NGC, **35** (b) Matt Mawson/Latitude/ Corbis, **36–37** Leonardo Mercon/VWPics/Redux, **38–39** (b) Joel Sartore/NGC, **39** (tr) Michelle Valberg/NGC, **40** (t) Annie Tritt Photography, **41** (tr) Daniel Etzold/Shutterstock, (b) Image Source/Getty Images, **42–43** Travis Dewitz/NGC, **44** Michael Pettigrew/iStockphoto, **45** Timothy Allen/ Getty Images, **46–47** Sandy Huffaker/The New York Time/Redux, **50** Kasha Slavner, **51** (tr) Toru Yamanaka/Getty Images, (b) anzlyldrm/Getty Images, **52–53** Patrick Dowd, **55** Kasha Salvner, **56–57** Ira Block/NGC, **58–59** (b) A9999 DB Rep of Maldives/Dol Ho/Corbis Wire/Corbis, **60** Sara Penryn Jones, (br) Andi Wollitz, **61** (tr) HorenkO/Shutterstock, (b) JetPack International, **62–63** Norbert Rosing/NGC, **65** Paul Nicklen/NGC, **66–67** NASA Images, **69** (tr) AF archive/Alamy, **70** (t) Mark Thiessen/NGC, (br) Emory Kristof/NGC, **71** Gabriel Bouys/AFP/Getty Images, **72–73** Gregory A. Harlin/NGC, **74** (bc) William West/AFP/Getty Images, **75** Kenneth Garrett/NGC, **76–77** Lam Yik Fei/Getty Images, **79** Religious Images/UIG/ Getty Images, **80** Zuma Press, **81** Romeo Ranoco/Reuters, **82–83** Action Plus/Aurora Photos, **85** Paul Nicklen, **86–87** Lyn Alweis/The Denver Post/Getty Images, **89** Dado Ruvic/Reuters, **90** Kris Krug, **91** Tim Boyle/Bloomberg/Getty Images, **92** (tl) Jason Edwards/Newspix/Getty Images, **92–93** Tim Wimborne/Reuters/Corbis, **95** Hannah Reyes, **96–97** Cory Richards/NGC, **98–99** Steven Watt/Reuters, **100** The Washington Post/ Getty Images, **101** John Eastcott/Yva Momatiuk/NGC, **102–103** Lynn Johnson, **105** Mark Stevenson/Alloy/Corbis, **106–107** David Brabyn/The New York Times/Redux, **108–109** Stanislaw Pytel/Digital Vision/Getty Images, **110** (t) PhotoAlto/James Hardy/Getty Images, (cr) Brian Harkin/The New York Times/Redux, **111** (tr) Lee319/Shutterstock, (b) Yoshikazu Tsuno/Getty Images, **112–113** Gianni Cipriano/The New York Times/Redux, **115** Catherine Karnow/NGC, **116–117** International Astronomical Union/NASA Astronomy Picture of the Day Collection/NASA Images, **117** (b) NASA Solarsystem Collection/ Nasa Images, **119** NASA, **120** NASA, **121** (tr) NASA, (br) Rhys Taylor/Stocktrek Images/Getty Images, **122–123** ESA/ Rosetta/Navcam, **125** (tl) (tr) (cl) (cr) NASA/JPL, (b) NASA/JPL-Caltech/MSSS

NGC = National Geographic Creative

Art Credits

8, 18, 28, 38, 48, 58, 68, 78, 88, 98, 108, 118, 126, 128, 129, 130 Raketshop, **26** Arcady/Shutterstock, **26, 30** Ecelop/ Shutterstock, **35** chartcameraman/Shutterstock, **72** Nikiteev_Konstantin/Shutterstock, Marie Nimrichterova/Shutterstock, **85** SoleilC/Shutterstock, Amornism/Shutterstock, Leremy/Shutterstock, VoodooDot/Shutterstock, **96** Mirinae/Shutterstock, pio3/ Shutterstock, Leremy/Shutterstock, **107** Kaissa/Shutterstock, Jennifer Gottschalk/Shutterstock, Abdurahman/Shutterstock, Goldenarts/Shutterstock, **115** Brothers Good/Shutterstock, Pensiri/Shutterstock

Acknowledgments

The authors and publisher would like to thank the following individuals and organizations who offered many helpful insights, ideas, and suggestions during the development of **Time Zones**.

Asia and Europe

Phil Woodall, Aoyama Gakuin Senior High School; **Suzette Buxmann**, Aston A+; **Wayne Fong**, Aston English; Berlitz China; Berlitz Germany; Berlitz Hong Kong; Berlitz Japan; Berlitz Singapore; **Anothai Jetsadu**, Cha-am Khunying Nuangburi School; **Rui-Hua Hsu**, Chi Yong High School; **Gary Darnell**, DEU Private School, Izmir; **Hwang Soon Hee, Irean Yeon, Junhee Im, Seungeun Jung**, Eun Seok Elementary School; **Hyun Ah Park**, Gachon University; **Hsi-Tzu Hung**, Hwa Hsia Institute of Technology; **Kate Sato**, Kitopia English School; **Daniel Stewart**, Kaisei Junior and Senior High School; **Haruko Morimoto, Ken Ip**, Mejiro Kenshin Junior and Senior High School; **Sovoan Sem**, Milky Way School; **Shu-Yi Chang**, Ming Dao High School; **Ludwig Tan**, National Institute of Education; **Tao Rui, Yuan Wei Hua**, New Oriental Education & Technology Group; **Tom Fast**, Okayama Gakugeikan High School; **Yu-Ping Luo**, Oriental Institute of Technology; **Jutamas**, Prakhanong Pittayalai School; **Akira Yasuhara**, Rikkyo Ikebukuro Junior and Senior High School; **Matthew Rhoda**, Sakuragaoka Junior and Senior High School; **Michael Raship, Nicholas Canales**, Scientific Education Group Co; **Andrew O'Brien**, Second Kyoritsu Girls Junior and Senior High School; **Atsuko Okada**, Shinagawa Joshi Gakuin Junior and Senior High School; **Sheila Yu**, Shin Min High School; **Stewart Dorward**, Shumei Junior and Senior High School; **Gaenor Hardy**, Star English Centres; **Philip Chandler, Thomas Campagna**, Tama University Meguro Junior and Senior High School; **Lois Wang**, Teachall English; **Iwao Arai, James Daly, Satomi Kishi**, Tokyo City University Junior and Senior High School; **Jason May**, Tokyo Seitoku University High School; **Amnoui Jaimipak**, Triamudomsuksapattanakarn Chiangrai School; **Jonee de Leon**, Universal English Center; **Thiwaphorn Tharawatcharasart**, Uthaiwitthayakhom School; **Richard Ascough**, Wayo Women's University; **Kirvin Andrew Dyer**, Yan Ping High School

The Americas

Allynne Fraemam, Flávia Carneiro, Jonathan Reinaux, Mônica Carvalho, ABA; **Antonio Fernando Pinho**, Academia De Idiomas; **Wilmer Escobar**, Academia Militar; **Adriana Rupp, Denise Silva, Jorge Mendes**, ACBEU; **Rebecca Gonzalez**, AIF Systems English Language Institute; **Camila Vidal Suárez, Adriana Yaffe, Andrea da Silva, Bruno Oliveri, Diego A. Fábregas Acosta, Fabiana Hernandez, Florencia Barrios, Ignacio Silveira Trabal, Lucía Greco Castro, Lucy Pintos, Silvia Laborde**, Alianza Cultural Uruguay Estados Unidos; **Adriana Alvarez**, ASICANA; **Corina C. Machado Correa, Silvia Helena R. D. Corrêa, Mariana M. Paglione Vedana**, Associacao Alumni; Berlitz, Colombia; Berlitz Mexico; Berlitz Peru; Berlitz US; **Simone Ashton**, Britanic Madalena; **Keith Astle**, Britanic Piedade; **Dulce Capiberibe**, Britanic Setúbal; **Matthew Gerard O'Conner**, Britanic Setúbal; **Viviane Remígio**, Britanic Setúbal; **Adriana da Silva, Ana Raquel F. F. Campos, Ebenezer Macario, Giselle Schimaichel, Larissa Platinetti, Miriam Alves Carnieletto, Selma Oliveira**, Centro Cultural Brasil Estados Unidos CCBEU; **Amiris Helena**, CCDA; **Alexandra Nancy Lake Sawada, Ana Tereza R. P. Moreira, Denise Helena Monteiro, Larissa Ferreria, Patricia Mckay Aronis**, CELLEP; **Claudia Patricia Gutierrez, Edna Zapata, Leslie Cortés, Silvia Elena Martinez, Yesid Londoño**, Centro Colombo Americano-Medellin; **Gabriel Villamar Then**, Centro Educativo los Prados; **Monica Lugo**, Centro Escolar Versalles; **Adriane Caldas, Simone Raupp, Sylvia Formoso**, Colégio Anchieta; **José Olavo de Amorim**, Colégio Bandeirantes; **Dionisio Alfredo Meza Solar**, Colegio Cultural I; **Madson Gois Diniz**, Colegio De Aplicação; **Ilonka Diaz, Melenie Gonzalez**, Colegio Dominico Espanol; **Laura Monica Cadena, Rebeca Perez**, Colegio Franco Ingles; **Jedinson Trujillo**, Colegio Guías; **Christophe Flaz, Isauro Sanchez Gutierrez**, Colegio Iglesa Bautista Fundamenta; **Ayrton Lambert**, Colégio Il Peretz; **Samuel Jean Baptiste**, Colegio Instituto Montessori; **Beatriz Galvez, Evelyn Melendez**, Colegio Los Olivos; **Carlos Gomez, Diana Herrera Ramirez, Diana Pedraza Aguirre, Karol Bibana Hutado Morales**, Colegio Santa Luisa; **Marta Segui Rivas**, Colegio Velmont; **Thays Ladosky**, DAMAS; **Amalia Vasquez, Ana Palencia, Fernando de Leon, Isabel Cubilla, Leonel Zapata, Lorena Chavarria, Maria Adames**, English Access Microscholarship Program; **Rosângela Duarte Dos Santos**, English Space; **Walter Junior Ribeiro Silva**, Friends Language Center; **Luis Reynaldo Frias**, Harvard Institute; **Carlos Olavo Queiroz Guimarães, Elisa Borges, Patricia Martins, Lilian Bluvol Vaisman, Samara Camilo Tomé Costa**, IBEU; **Gustavo Sardo, João Carlos Queiroz Furtado, Rafael Bastos, Vanessa Rangel**, IBLE; **Graciela Martin**, ICANA (BELGRANO); **Carlos Santanna, Elizabeth Gonçalves**, ICBEU; **Inês Greve Milke, João Alfredo Bergmann**, Instituto Cultural Brasileiro Norte-Americano; **Tarsis Perez**, ICDA-Instituto Cultural Dominico Americano; **Cynthia Marquez, Guillermo Cortez, Ivan Quinteros, Luis Morales R, Melissa Lopez, Patricia Perez, Rebeca de Arrue, Rebeca Martinez de Arrue**, Instituto Guatemalteco Americano; **Renata Lucia Cardoso**, Instituto Natural de Desenvolvimento Infantil; **Graciela Nobile**, Instituto San Diego; **Walter Guevara**, Pio XII; **Juan Omar Valdez**, Professional Training Systems; **Carlos Carmona, Eugenio Altieri, Regan Albertson**, Progressive English Services; **Raul Billini**, Prolingua; **Juan Manuel Marin, Luisa Fecuanda Infort, Maria Consuelo Arauijo**, Providencia; **Carmen Gehrke**, Quatrum, Porto Alegre; **Rodrigo Rezende**, Seven; **Lcuciano Joel del Rosario**, St. José School; **Sabino Morla**, UASD; **Silvia Regina D'Andrea**, União Cultural Brasil-Estados Unidos; **Ruth Salomon-Barkemeyer**, Unilínguas Sao Leopoldo; **Anatalia Souza, Livia Rebelo**, UNIME-Ingles Para Criancas-Salvador; **Andrei dos Santos Cunha, Brigitte Mund, Gislaine Deckmann, Jeane Blume Cortezia, Rosana Gusmão**, Unisinos; **Diego Pérez**, Universidad de Ibague; **Beatriz Daldosso Felippe**, U.S. Idiomas Universe School

David Bohlke would like to thank the entire editorial team at National Geographic Learning for their dedication to producing such stimulating and engaging learning materials. He would also like to thank Jennifer Wilkin and the rest of *Time Zones* author team for making the first edition such a success.